Bettie Page

The Life of a Pin-Up Legend

FEBRUARY 1955

Sun	Mon	Tue	Wed	Thu	Fri	Sat
		1	2	3	4	5
6	7	8	9	10	11	12
13	14	15	16	17	18	19
20	21	22	23	24	25	26
27	28					

Sun-Kissed Siren ★ A real girl of nature is 22-year-old Bettie Page, of Nashville, relaxing on a Florida beach. Trained from childhood to be a dancer, she suddenly decided to throw her steps to the wind and become an actress. Bettie started her theatrical life as an ingenue in summer stock — as you can see she's well equipped.

Bettie Page

The Life of a Pin-Up Legend

By Karen Essex
and James L. Swanson

Foreword by Bettie Page

General Publishing Group
Los Angeles

Publisher: W. Quay Hays
Editorial Director: Peter L. Hoffman
Managing Editor: Colby Allerton
Art Director: Kurt Wahlner
Interior Designs: Dave Stevens and Kurt Wahlner
Production Director: Trudihope Schlomowitz
Prepress Manager: Bill Castillo
Production Assistants: Gus Dawson and Russel Lockwood

Original Edition
Production Director: Nadeen Torio
Production Assistants: Tom Archibeque, Michael Lira, Alan Peak, Brad Slepack

For information:
General Publishing Group, Inc.
2701 Ocean Park Boulevard
Santa Monica, CA 90405

Essex, Karen.
    Bettie Page : the life of a pin-up legend / by Karen Essex and James L. Swanson;
        p.   cm.
    ISBN 1-57544-080-6 (paperback)
    I. Page, Bettie. 2. Models (Persons)–United States–Biography.
I. Swanson, James L. II. Page, Bettie. III. Title
HD9999.M642P344   1995
659.1'52-dc20
[B]   95-31828
                             CIP

Printed in the USA by RR Donnelley and Sons Company
10 9 8 7 6 5 4 3 2 1

Table of Contents

October 10, 1995

Dear friends,

This book is a journey through my memories. Memories of sitting on my grandmother's stoop as a little girl almost seventy years ago. Memories of an orphanage. Memories of photographs taken long ago, of friends not seen in many years. For this book, I went back to the very beginning and traveled forward to the present day. So many recollections, bitter and sweet, have come back to me. Karen and James have written the real story, both the good and the bad. They set the record straight, and that's what I wanted.

I never would have believed that in 1995, so many years after the modeling days, I would be telling my story. I thought that surely I would be long forgotten. I am flattered by your interest in my life, and astonished that you still care about me, though sometimes all this attention is still not quite real to me. Many of you are young enough to be my grandchildren.

I was not trying to be shocking, or to be a pioneer. I wasn't trying to change society, or to be ahead of my time. I didn't think of myself as liberated, and I don't believe that I did anything important. I was just myself. I didn't know any other way to be, or any other way to live. If my photographs speak to you, then I am happy. If I am remembered today, it is because you, the reader, see something in me that I never saw in myself.

My last public appearance was in 1957, nearly 40 years ago. I have received many kind invitations to come forward and host special events, or to appear on television, but I will not do that. Please remember me as I was. I hope that you understand. I am content now. I enjoy my privacy and my simple life. I have no regrets. To friends new and old, I thank you all.

Love,
Bettie Page

Acknowledgments

Bob Schultz, pin-up scholar extraordinaire, placed the best Bettie Page collection in the world at our disposal and flew to Los Angeles whenever we needed his expertise. Bob, a member of Bettie's small circle of friends, helps keep the myth alive.

Dave Stevens, artist, collector and keeper of the flame, lent us his art, advice, layout skills, studio and knowledge of 1950s pop culture. Dave helped revive the Bettie Page myth with his landmark publication, *The Rocketeer*. Today, he enjoys the trust and friendship of the woman behind the legend.

Unselfishly, Dave and Bob dropped their own plans and projects whenever we asked for their help. With good humor and in the spirit of friendship they gave us their all. We could never have written this book without them.

Elizabeth Snead navigated us through the fashion world and shared her insight into the Bettie Page phenomenon. For her friendship, for help in Paris and New York and for long dinners and memorable conversation, we thank her.

Special thanks to Quay Hays for publishing the book, to Murray Fisher for invaluable editorial advice and to Gaston Moraga for going above and beyond the call of duty when we needed help.

We also thank the others who helped make this book possible: Art Amsie, Joe Anderko, Joey Arias, Joel Beren, Robert Blue, Randy Brooke, Stuart Cameron, Tony Campo, Tim Carrigan, Naomi Caryl, Jung Choi, Amber Clapp, D. Dexter Correa, Michael Cunningham, Janice Dickinson, Ti Eastman, Andrew Epstein, Rüdiger Fliess, Gregory & Christina Gaymont, Marc Greenblum, Herbert Hancock, Shalom Harlow, Hugh M. Hefner, Eva Herzigova, Phalen G. "Chuck" Hurewitz, Mary Ann Jetton, Lee Kaplan, Paula Klaw, Katy K at Ranch Dressing, Carol LeFlufy, Bill Liebowitz, Herb Lichtenstein, Peter Lindbergh, Lisa Lovatt-Smith, Elle MacPherson, Robert & Charlotte Martis, Debi Mazar, Richard Merkin, Amy Newman, Maggie Newman, David Oates, Todd Oldham, Olivia, Jack and Kevin Page, Gary Anthony Paruolo, Lauren Purcell, Ken Ritchie, J. B. Rund, Albert Sanchez, Chris Schramm, Larry Schubert, Howard Shapiro, Larry Shell, Eric Stanton, Tommy Stanziola, Chantal Thomass, Ellen von Unwerth, Albert Watson, Donald Whitney and Addison Yeaman, Jr.

Karen Essex and James L. Swanson

I'd like to thank friends and family, who offered me unqualified love and support; particularly Olivia Fox, Keith Fox who takes care of her while I work and Mikal Gilmore who long ago told me the legend of Bettie Page and encouraged me to write about her. Many thanks to Kit Rachlis and R. J. Smith, formerly of the *L.A. Weekly*, for knowing a good story when they heard one and for their editorial guidance.   K. E.

With special thanks to Lennart, Dianne and Denise Swanson for unwavering support, and in memory of my grandmother Elizabeth, hipster and iconoclast, who nonetheless longed for the day when I would finish this book, give up pin-up models and become a "real lawyer" again.   J. L. S.

Introduction

I was never the girl next door.
—Bettie Page

She couldn't imagine why we wanted to write a book about her. The "modeling days," as she called them, ended decades ago. "Who wants to read about me? I'm not important. All I did was pose for some pictures."

Was she kidding? In the Fifties those pictures rocked America. They violated sexual taboos, provoked the wrath of a congressional committee and made Bettie Page the greatest pin-up in history before she vanished without a trace in 1957 at the height of her fame. Today, because of those pictures, she is a legend, influencing contemporary style, fashion and photography from Soho to Paris. She inspires supermodels, photographers, designers, artists and rock stars worldwide — not to mention fans from her heyday and those young enough to be her grand-children. With more magazine appearances than Marilyn Monroe and Cindy Crawford com-bined, she is the model of the century, yet she remains one of its best-kept secrets. Like James Dean and Monroe, she left us early; like all the great ones, she left us a look and a mystique that have endured the test of time.

Bettie Page embodied the stereotypical wholesomeness of the Fifties and the hidden sexu-ality straining beneath the surface. She was the ultimate model of the post war pin-up era — the girl next door, naughty and nice. As America grappled with the duality of its sexual long-ings, Bettie Page ripped through layers of repression, the harbinger of a more liberated time just around the corner. Her fresh-faced beauty was the perfect camouflage for what lurked beneath her veneer — the exotic, whip-snapping dark angel. In Bettie Page, forbidden long-ings were made safe by an ideal American girl.

She was one of the first centerfolds for a fledgling men's magazine called *Playboy*. Without apology or shame, she posed nude — a profane act of rebellion in her time. More daring yet, she posed for fetish and bondage scenarios, which earned her a fanatical underground following.

It began with the fetching black bangs and lush raven hair. Flawless skin and dazzling blue eyes. An eternal smile implying infinite possibilities. Sexual possibilities. An athletic body that never lost its luscious curves. A taut waist, buoyant breasts and round, firm feminine hips barely covered by a scant bikini. On the dark side, the accouterments of seduction — black gloves clothing hands that beckon, fishnet stockings on long legs, garter belts with nothing under-neath, defiant black heels, and sometimes even a whip or a collar. A visage that is amused: She's caught you looking, spying on her private moment, but she doesn't mind. She is charmed by your intrusion. Is she teasing you? Or are you invited?

The real Bettie Page never understood that she had done something important. During her 38-year self-imposed exile from public life, in the wake of her notoriety, she became, unbe-knownst to her, a worldwide phenomenon. For decades, Page cultists, as well as journalists, publishers, photographers and the curious, tried unsuccessfully to lure her out of seclusion. When bondage apparel became fashion, her photos and her look were right back in the main-stream along with the garments she used to wear. Bettie glorified fetish, seduction and voyeurism long before Versace, Gaultier, Dolce & Gabbana and other top designers. On the runways and on the street, women of style emulate her look. She is the dark Monroe, precursor to Madonna, third member of a triptych of American style and sexuality.

But where had she gone? She was always elusive, even before she vanished. She inspired Hugh Hefner, but he had never been able to meet her. An infatuated Howard Hughes summoned her, but she would not come. After she was gone, Gay Talese sought her for his book about the sexual revolution, *Thy Neighbor's Wife*, but he couldn't find her. Willie Morris pined for her in one of *Esquire*'s "Women We Love" issues. While her whereabouts remained a mystery, rumors about her fate spread. Some claimed she fled the country; others said she was dead. Through the decades, public and private appeals for Bettie Page went unanswered.

Then, in 1991, an article appeared in *USA Today* about the missing pin-up queen and the growing Page phenomenon — posters, T-shirts, buttons, model kits, a comic book and motion picture called *The Rocketeer* — surrounding a woman no one had seen for decades.

In late 1992 *Lifestyles of the Rich and Famous* aired a segment with a man who said he was Bettie Page's brother. It included a brief audiotape of a woman saying that she was the real Bettie Page — alive and well, amazed at her popularity and refusing to be seen. Karen Essex, a journalist who had written about her, contacted Bettie's brother, only to be told that he'd engaged James Swanson, a writer and attorney who represents artists, models and photographers. Inundated with requests from merchandisers, producers, fans, cranks and opportunists, the family hired James to protect Bettie from the consequences of her fame.

He began working for Bettie without meeting her. He was told that there was no point in meeting her, and little in talking to her. She'd already said the last thing she ever intended to say about the old days. It became clear that someone was going to write a book about Bettie, with or without her cooperation. Bettie remained uninterested because she believed people wouldn't care about her story. But James began sending Bettie recent newspaper and magazine clippings about her. She liked Karen's article from the *L.A. Weekly*.

James and Karen decided to meet. We discovered mutual interests: history both ancient and modern, a romance with the Civil War and lost causes — and a genuine concern for Bettie Page. For almost 40 years, she had received nothing while others exploited her fame and her face by selling photos and unlicensed merchandise. Though she lived modestly on Social Security, Bettie Page was neither greedy nor bitter. But she needed help. We decided to write a book and share the proceeds with her, if she would allow us.

Finally, Bettie agreed to talk, but she didn't want to see us, meaning that she didn't want us to see her. She said she was old now, and no longer beautiful. If we came looking for the woman in the photos, we would not find her; the magic that survives in the pictures died in her a long time ago. She didn't want to disappoint. And wouldn't we be wasting our time, traveling across the country to write a book that no one would read about a woman no one remembered? We reminded her that others were searching for her and planning to write their own books. Shouldn't her biography be based on her recollections? Reluctantly, she told us to come — but without cameras.

As we drove into the California desert for our rendezvous, giddy with the thought that we would be the first writers to meet America's lost pin-up queen, we asked many questions. Was she a feisty sexual renegade or a broken and bitter recluse? Did she see herself as a victim? What was the source of her mystique? How was it that for the past four decades, she had become more and more famous? Most important, how could we be sure it was her?

In the end, we didn't need identification; we knew from the moment we saw her. She opened the door and we felt the thrill of recognition. The same eyes, the same smile, and even the same long hair, though now gray. The spirit in the old photos still radiated from the sporty 70-year-old woman standing before us wearing the famous bangs.

Bettie Page is a soft-spoken, unpretentious woman who has retained her Southern accent and manners. During our week with her, she spoke candidly about her life and demonstrated an uncanny memory of past events. As she reviewed photos she hadn't seen in more than 40 years, she remembered the dresses and the bikinis she had made, names and places from her past and what she was thinking as she sat on her grandmother's stoop as a small child. She seemed shy at first. But once she relaxed, she was chatty and funny — and keenly interested in judging whether a picture of her was good or bad.

The real Bettie Page is a lot like the Bettie Page we imagine in our collective fantasies. She communicates many of the same characteristics: authenticity, sweetness, a sense of fun, openness, accessibility, jauntiness. She is an intelligent woman with a great interest in books and films, an avid reader mostly of history and biography. She does not seem like the kind of person who would hide herself away for decades.

Bettie told us her story right up to the present. She told us of her hard early life in Tennessee, her family, her girlhood dreams, her victories and her traumas. She told us about her lovers and her husbands, and about the day a photographer discovered her walking on a Coney Island beach — the event that changed her life and immortalized her. She told us what she did and where she went when she turned her back on it all. Then she apologized for not living a more fascinating life. "I guess you'll have to invent things about me to make it interesting. Well, I trust you. Let your imaginations run wild!"

So this book is part biography, part scrapbook and part history of a legend. It is the story of a woman ahead of her time who never set out to be famous. She embarked on a personal journey and inadvertently became a mythic symbol of sexuality. She takes no credit for her impact and offers no explanation for her iconic status. In her view, she was chosen randomly, a delightful but puzzling accident. "I haven't the foggiest notion why I'm so popular," she says. But the meaning of Bettie Page far exceeds the importance of the events of her life, or her own understanding of her fame.

We set out to solve the twin mysteries of her disappearance and her appeal, but we encountered greater mysteries along the way: the hypnotic power and mystique of a sex symbol; the complex nature of sexuality, both now and then; the duality of American desire. Her story, her career and what she represents tell us about our longings, past and present.

Karen Essex

James L. Swanson

Santa Monica, California

PART ONE

Prelude to a Pin-Up

Bettie Page sitting on the steps of her home across the street from the state capitol in Nashville. "This is me, about 12 years old, in my yellow organdy dress that Momma bought me for graduation from junior high." Opposite page: Bettie at six, surrounded by her grandmother and five siblings.

The Early Years
1923 to 1936

On the evening of April 21, 1923, Walter Roy Page, a 27-year-old auto mechanic from Jackson, Tennessee, and his wife, the former Edna Mae Pirtle, 23 and a housewife, attended the late show at a theater in downtown Nashville. The couple's two-year-old son, Billy, slept in his father's arms. He would have preferred, perhaps, the lap of his mother, but in the last stages of pregnancy with a second child, she couldn't accommodate him. At 11 o'clock — the movie was not yet over — Edna felt the familiar contractions, and they left the theater, returning to their small brick home several blocks away. They contacted a midwife or doctor — no one remembers which — one "S. Cowan" according to the birth certificate, and on April 22 at three o'clock in the morning, the couple's second child, Betty Mae, was born. Perhaps with those early contractions, Bettie's lifelong passion for cinema was born. "I was almost born in a movie theater. I wonder if that's why I've always loved the movies so much."

No one said she was an outstandingly beautiful child — that came later. At the time she was just a cute, even-tempered little girl who was no trouble to her mother, and who rarely cried. She was number two out of an eventual six — a quiet baby born with a full head of brown hair. A year later brother Jimmy was born, followed by sister Goldie and brother Jack. Finally baby sister Joyce completed the family. Early on, Betty and Jimmy began to spell their names "Bettie" and "Jimmie."

Despite the arrival of a healthy new baby every year or two and the camaraderie among the children, the Page home wasn't happy. The couple fought often and the topic was always the same — other women. "My father was a womanizer. He could never get enough of women and enough of sex," Bettie says, reflecting on those early years. "My mother

Above: Bettie wearing her Easter dress in Nashville's Centennial Park, and with her sister Joyce. Below: Bettie (top center) with her brothers and sisters on the stoop of their house.

was just a louse."

When Edna was eight months pregnant with Jimmie — and had two small children to care for — Roy locked her out of the house one night in the pouring rain because she didn't feel up to having sex. He didn't allow her back into the house until she agreed to comply with his wishes. "I always disliked him for that whenever I've had to think about it. It was very cruel. He never drank or smoked or took drugs or anything like that, and yet he was woman-crazy."

Despite the problems, Edna remained in the marriage. Bettie believes that her mother had little choice. She had married young, and out of necessity. Her own mother had died when Edna was only three years old, and for years she was shuffled from one brother or sister to another. With a wedding would come, at least, a home of her own. Still, Bettie believes the price Edna paid was too high.

By the late 1920s Roy Page had five children to feed. During the Depression work for a local mechanic was scarce, so the family took to the road to find him a job. They traveled throughout the South and Southwest stopping in Texas, Arkansas and Oklahoma. One of Bettie's earliest memories was watching in astonishment as a house in Tulsa was moved down the street. She was seven years old, and shocked that something that seemed so permanent could be lifted up and taken away. The scene foreshadowed Bettie's own experience.

When Roy couldn't find work in Tulsa — and couldn't pay rent on the house the family had settled into — they were evicted, put out on the street with no money and nowhere to go. Bettie recalls them standing on the sidewalk with their possessions at their feet, wondering what they would do in this strange city where they knew no one,

wouldn't have stayed with him as long as she did except that she was pregnant with one child after another every year or so. They should never have married. They argued all the time, mostly about his other women. Momma was very faithful, but he

and had exhausted their meager resources. There was no one to call, nowhere to live, no work available. Edna stood with her five children waiting for her husband to do something.

Desperate, Roy left, promising to return with a solution. He stole the first car he could find to get his family back to Nashville. There relatives might help out, as Southerners, no matter how poor, usually do. The family piled in and hit the road for Tennessee. Roy managed to get them back home to his mother's house, but then his luck ran out. The stolen car belonged to a deputy sheriff in Tulsa who tracked him down the very next day. Roy Page spent two years in the Atlanta penitentiary.

Edna and the children lived with his mother, Corilla Page, in her large, ramshackle home in downtown Nashville while he was in prison. The elder Mrs. Page saved the family, according to Bettie. "I don't know what Momma would've done with all of us if hadn't been for Grandmother." The nation had not yet emerged from the Depression, and there was little work for an unskilled woman.

Though she was only eight years old, Bettie played the role of eldest daughter. Dutiful and competent, she did most of the chores and cared for her younger brothers and sisters. She recalls with lingering distaste the number of diapers she had to change.

Bettie discovered early on that she was a loner, learning to entertain herself with her active imagination and a strong creative streak. When she wasn't helping her mother, she spent endless hours drawing horses, a typical obsession of dreamy young girls. To entertain her younger sisters, Bettie invented "the beauty contest game." With no money for art supplies,

"This is me, walking down Church Street past the place where the boys used to sit and ogle the girls. I'm wearing an old blue coat of Momma's and a skirt that she cut down to fit me. I used to wear a lot of hand-me-downs."

Above: Bettie at the Pittsburgh Zoo in 1947, in a photo taken by her sister Goldie. Right: Summer 1941. Goldie and Bettie at the entrance to Shelby Park in Nashville.

she discovered that the touch of her fingers on the porcelain cabinet doors in the kitchen resulted in images. She drew beautiful girls using only the oil on her fingers, shadowing in the figures and features on the cabinet doors. "I would draw faces, and my sisters and I would have a contest to decide which ones had the prettiest eyes, nose, mouth, hair and costume, and things like that. We spent a lot of time doing that, and Momma didn't care as long as I

cleaned it off after." Though she showed an early interest in glamour, Bettie claims that she never dreamed as a child of becoming a model.

Meanwhile, Roy Page used his prison sentence to advantage, working as a mechanic in the machine shop and saving all his earnings. After the disaster in Tulsa, he wanted to never be dependent on others again. He had a new plan, one that promised his large family self-sufficiency and security. In 1932 Roy Page bought a 48 acre farm on the Memphis Highway, 30 miles west of Nashville. Bettie was nine years old, and the children enrolled in the local school two miles away in tiny Gingo, Tennessee — now vanished — six miles from Kingston Springs. With no money for shoes, they walked barefoot to school. Soon they found ways to skip out with impunity,

"I had my hair permed in high school. How I hated it! I couldn't wait for it to grow out, so I cut it off."

discovering other rural activities that were simply more fun. "A whole lot of the time we'd come home for lunch and wouldn't go back in the afternoon. We'd go down to the creek and play until four o'clock in the afternoon, and then go home. We never told Momma or Daddy about it, of course."

In the absence of money for toys and other costly amusements, the children invented their own entertainment. "We were so poor, we didn't have any toys at all," Bettie says. "We'd get a couple of feathers from the chickens and blow on them and duel each other with them to see who could keep them going the longest. We called it 'Fighting Feathers.' When we got tired of that, we'd play horses. We'd get a big long stick and put a bridle on it made out of string and corn tassels for the mane and have races up and down the dirt road. We also had a lot of running races, and I could always beat Jimmie and Billy both. I was a good runner when I was a child."

But there was little time for games. The land was rocky and hard to plant in, and water had to be hauled up a hill from the closest spring. The largest share of chores fell upon the oldest three children — Billy,

Above: Bettie and Goldie at Shelby Park. Left: Bettie, 18, Goldie, 16, and Joyce, 11, at the park, making like chorus girls.

Bettie with an early beau. "He was a neighbor boy. I don't think I ever even kissed him."

Bettie and Jimmie. Their father promised to pay his children five cents for each bucket of rocks they removed, five cents for each bucket of water hauled up the hill and five cents for watering a row of sweet potatoes. Each child performed the chores dutifully, carefully recording every chore performed. Within a year Bettie and Jimmie had worked so hard they had amassed wages in excess of $300 each. But Roy never paid them. "I asked him one day when I was about thirteen years old, 'Daddy, when are you going to pay us the money you owe us?' He just laughed and said, 'Now, Chummy,' — he always called me Chummy — 'you didn't really expect me to give you any money for that work, did you?'"

The memory still angers her. "Imagine, as hard as we worked, little kids picking up rocks and hauling water up a big hill! And he just laughed and thought it was funny. I hated him for a long time after that. That was a terrible thing to do to little children." That year on the farm also introduced Bettie to romance. She had her first crush on a boy, a 15-year-old named Clarence Daubenspeck, who lived with his family across the creek from the Page farm. "I was nine years old and I thought I was in love." She lost all affection for him, however, when he wounded her in a rock fight. "One day Jimmie and I and Clarence and his cousin Alvin started having a rock fight across the creek. Clarence hit me on the left hand with a rock, and I got so mad at him, I called him every name in the book. I never liked him after that." But 10 years later she cried when she read in the newspaper that her childhood friend had died in World War II.

The family's dream of independence on the farm was short-lived. A 15-year-old girl named Rosie, from a family of 17 children, turned up pregnant. When she named the father — Roy Page — the girl's father came to the Pages' door with a shotgun while Roy ran out the back and into the woods. Edna, humiliated and furious, threw the family dishes at him as he ran. She packed up and hitchhiked the 30 miles back to Nashville, promising her children she would send for them soon. She was true to her word. Two by two, the children came to live with her.

But Edna's divorce didn't make her life any easier. In 1933 America was still steeped in the Depression. To make ends meet, she worked as a hairdresser and took in as much laundry as she could handle at night. The children understood their mother's predicament and helped out as much as possible. Yet Edna lashed out at the girls, telling them that they were a lot of trouble. Besides, she hadn't wanted so many children anyway. More painfully, she told them that she had never wanted daughters at all. But Bettie believes that Edna spoke in frustration. She admires the way her mother kept the family together against insurmountable odds, seeing all the children through school, while Roy didn't contribute a cent to their welfare.

When Edna ran out of money, unable to take care of them, she put her three girls in an orphanage for a year while she went on working. During that time the Page daughters invented another game, "Program," that foreshadowed Bettie's future. All the girls sat in a circle, with one in the center who mimicked the poses of movie stars and models in magazines and newspapers. The girls could also make a request of the girl in the center — to dance, sing a song or perform in some other way. The girls often asked Bettie to do the hula. "I suppose I first learned how to pose from playing 'Program' as a child," Bettie says.

She was 10 years old when she entered the orphanage and 11 when the girls returned home. With Edna working as a hairdresser, Bettie and her sisters began experimenting with hairdos and makeup. "My mother was very beautiful. Everybody always said she had a queenly appearance. By the time I was eleven or twelve, I was plucking my eyebrows like Momma, trying to look like her." The other girls followed suit, wearing their mother's makeup and imitating the expressions of their favorite stars.

Roy Page returned to Nashville, finished with Rosie and the farm. Desperate for money, Edna rented him a room in the basement of her house. "We were so poor," Bettie remembers, "that we were lucky to get an orange in our Christmas stockings. Momma had only a third-grade education, and she wasn't trained to do anything. She did everything all by herself. The only help she ever had was that every Christmas we would get a box of food from a welfare organization."

Perhaps Edna thought Roy might help out, and that the children would benefit by having their father at home again. But if she knew what he was about to do to Bettie, she wouldn't have let him in the door. When her daughter turned 13, Roy began to abuse her sexually. He bribed her with dimes to go to movies — which he knew was her passion — if she allowed him to be sexual with her. Having already impregnated one teenager, he was careful not to have actual intercourse with her, but he insisted that she let him please himself in other ways. Bettie, a very naive 13, had no idea what he was doing — if it was right or wrong, good or bad. Her mother had never talked to her about sex. She was so innocent that later in the year, when she began to menstruate, she thought she was dying.

Bettie submitted to her father's wishes and told no one — for the next 59 years. "Like a fool," she says now, "I probably would have done anything just to go see cowboy movies." Though she was a child obeying her father, she, like many victims of sexual abuse, assumed the guilt for "allow-

Above: Bettie with her sister-in-law Gladys. Left: With a family friend at her father's house in East Nashville.

ing" it to happen. For years Bettie didn't think much about the episodes with her father. Only when she got older did she come to understand what had happened, and she hated him for it.

It seemed like Bettie was living alone inside a big family. Edna was too busy to take an interest in her, and she doesn't recall sharing her hopes and dreams with any of her siblings. During this troubling adolescence, she turned to a local community center where she learned to cook and to sew — a skill she later used making her own bikinis — and to play the piano. In the evenings, away from the noise of a house-

hold of children, she went to the center to do homework and to read. Unlike many children at this early stage of life, she was entirely self-motivated. Already she had highly developed interests. "I was never smarter than other children, but I studied all the time, which was why my grades were so high," she says modestly. She was preoccupied with academics rather than the usual early teenage girl's obsession: boys. Bettie knew that her ticket out of poverty was education.

Bettie, brother Jimmie and sister Goldie in Shelby Park. "There I am with that horrible $1.50 permanent!"

BETTIE PAGE

Top: Bettie in the yard of her father and stepmother's Nashville cottage on West Douglas Avenue. "My step-mother grew beautiful flowers, plants and vines." Left: Bettie at 18 on her mother's front lawn on Carter Lane. "That old house didn't even have a bathroom. It only had an outhouse. But it did have beautiful petunias." Right: Bettie holding a chicken.

CO. EDITOR

Bettie Page

Swan Emerging
1936 to 1940

High school opened up a new world to Bettie. Determined to win the full scholarship to Vanderbilt University that was awarded to the class valedictorian, she threw herself into both scholastics and extracurricular activities. While other girls fantasized about getting through high school so they could marry the boy of their dreams, Bettie dreamed about the scholarship and the opportunities it promised.

It's astonishing that she had time to study at all. The 1940 Hume-Fogg High School yearbook paints a portrait of Bettie Page as the ultimate golden girl — an achiever who excelled in everything she did. As a member and program director of the Dramatics Club, she performed in many of the school's productions, including roles as Lady MacBeth in *MacBeth* and Kate Pettigrew in *Berkeley Square*. She served as regimental sponsor for the ROTC for three high schools in Nashville; secretary-treasurer of the Student Council; co-editor of both the school newspaper, *The Fogg-Horn*, and the yearbook, *The Echo*. Her classmates voted her the "Girl Most Likely to Succeed" and when pondering what to will to her, the verdict was "Nothing. She already has everything." Though she has no memory of ever wanting to sing professionally, she said in the yearbook that her goal was to be a singer with a big-band orchestra — an aspiration that amuses her today because she swears that she

Student Council member, 1939 (center, front row).

cannot sing. The class prediction for Bettie for the year 1970 was that she would be preparing for her greatest role — as Ninotchka — opposite Mickey Rooney.

Her peers may have believed that she had everything, but it was far from true. Neither Edna nor Roy was involved in Bettie's high school life. Perhaps they didn't value education because neither advanced beyond the third grade. Ignorant of Bettie's school life and achievements, they knew nothing of her goal to win the scholarship to Vanderbilt. "They really didn't care if we went to school or not," Bettie claims.

Although Edna didn't attend her school plays or take an interest in any of her activities, she controlled her daughter's social life. She enforced one hard and fast rule: no dating, not even to the senior prom. Bettie obeyed her mother and sneaked out only once to meet a boy at a movie. She recalls having been quite content to stay home: "I don't think I would have dated much even if Momma would have allowed it. But I think it was cruel of her not to even let me go to the prom."

While Edna refused to let Bettie go out with boys, Momma had her own boyfriend in his early 20s. Bettie never liked him, but he had designs on her, though she was only 16. One day when she walked home from school, he tried to force her into his car. Bettie knew what he wanted and refused to get in. As she fought him off, her brother Jack, then 12 years old, rode by on his bike and told Edna that he had just seen Bettie getting into the man's car. When Bettie got home her mother flew into a rage of sexual jealousy, ripping off her favorite sweater and clawing her breasts viciously. Running out of the house to escape injury, Bettie was banned from her mother's home,

Above: Program chairman of the College Club, 1940.
Below: Student Council, sophomore year.

HALL OF FAME

Top: "Girl Most Likely to Succeed." Bettie's 1940 yearbook profile. Above: Girl Reporter, junior year, 1939. Opposite page: With Edna Page.

and lived during her senior year with her father and his new wife, Lulu, who was protective and kind and welcomed her.

Bettie and her mother reconciled after Edna dumped the young lover. Bettie understood that Edna's hard life cost her her looks and her youth when she was still young. "I didn't hold the incident against Momma," Bettie says. "She had been a beautiful woman when she was young, but she had six children when she only wanted half that number, and she had to raise them by herself." Surrounded by beautiful daughters and an unfaithful husband, Edna never liked or trusted other women. "Momma never had a girlfriend in her life," Bettie laments.

Bettie's efforts to win the scholarship to Vanderbilt ended in disappointment. She received a B in art when she skipped a class to rehearse for a play, and missed being valedictorian by one-quarter of a grade point. Instead of the full scholarship to a prestigious university, she received a $100 scholarship to George Peabody College, a four-year teacher's college. Bettie lost the one dream on which she had staked all her hopes for the future: "I was completely crushed after that."

As salutatorian, Bettie looked forward to delivering the opening address at the graduation exercises, where the girls had to wear evening gowns. "We were so poor that of course I didn't have a long gown," she reflects. "I kept asking my father to buy me one, but he put it off until the night before graduation. That Saturday night we took a bus downtown, and he bought me a dress and some shoes — but I accidentally left the bag with the dress in it on the counter at Morris's Department Store. I thought my father had it. We hurried back, but they were closed. I stared through the window at the package. I was just heartbroken."

All night Bettie lay in bed sick with a cold, devastated that she might not be allowed to attend her own graduation. Then she had an idea. "Two hours before graduation, I went downtown to the YWCA. I knocked on doors asking girls who lived there if they would let me borrow an evening gown. A very generous-hearted girl let me have a pretty white organdy dress. Luckily, it fit me just fine, so I was able to graduate. But I was miserable up on the stage. You see, we had such poor food at my house — we didn't get many vitamins, and no vitamin C at all — and I had a terrible cold all year. In June it was very bad. All I wanted to do was to get up and go to the restroom and cough."

Illness notwithstanding, Bettie delivered "Looking Forward," an optimistic speech she wrote about the future. Her mother didn't even attend the ceremony.

College Girl
1940 to 1946

Opposite page: Goldie and Bettie. Left: Edna and Bettie Page.

In 1940 career options for women were limited to secretary, teacher or wife. Bettie Page tried all three — simultaneously. Just before high school graduation she met a local sports star, William Neal, two years older than her. One day as she walked near Shelby Park memorizing a speech for a debate, she saw a small roadster turn the corner. "I heard a voice call out, 'Hey, beautiful! Are there any more at home like you?' That's how I met Billy Neal. He had been an outstanding football and basketball player at East High School. That impressed me."

For the next year and a half Bettie attended Peabody College and dated Billy Neal. "He taught me how to dance," she remembers. "I've been doing it since." She worked her way through school as secretary to Dr. Alfred Leland Crabb, a noted professor and author of three historical novels about the Civil War: *Dinner at Belmont, Supper at the Maxwell House* and *Breakfast at the Hermitage.* Bettie typed all three manuscripts working either from his handwritten notes on yellow legal pads or from dictation. "The punctuation was mine," she says, and recalls discussing ideas for the books with him as he constructed them. Crabb and his wife lived in an antebellum home in Nashville. Bettie visited the Crabbs on weekends, sometimes sleeping in their large guest room in a big four-poster bed on a huge feather mattress. "Mrs. Crabb would spoil me, laying out towels for me, running my bath, treating

Peabody Players

On Friday and Saturday nights, March 3 and 4, the Peabody Players presented a very successful three-act comedy entitled *Brief Music.* A civilian-soldier audience of unexpected numbers applauded the players for three curtain calls after each performance in the Demonstration School Auditorium.

Every member of the all-girl cast played her part with originality and naturalness. Jane Dabney as "Drizzle" and Virginia Alley as "Spiff" were outstanding in the leading roles, but Edith Feigenbaum as "Rosey" stole the show. Mary Knight as "Lovey," Bettie Page as "Maggie," Corynne Shockley as "Minnie," and Elizabeth Roller as "Jinx" all gave fine performances. Special credit for the success of the play went to Dorothy Waldrip, Peabody senior, who directed it.

Below: Bettie in the Peabody Players' *Love From A Stranger.* **Her review in** *The Peabody Reflector* **said, "As a silly, none-too-bright maid, Bettie Page proved her mettle as an actress."**

me like I was her own little child."

As in her high school days, Bettie compiled a dazzling array of extracurricular activities. She joined the Peabody Players, the campus dramatics club, which elected her secretary for the 1943-44 term. She acted in at least seven plays at the college, and performed in *Ah Wilderness!,* based on the novel by Willa Cather, at the Community Playhouse. Fascinated with mysteries and ghost stories, she also wrote a 15-minute play for the Peabody Players Radio Guild, which was about a secret room in an old house.

In December 1941, during Bettie's sophomore year at Peabody, Japan bombed Pearl Harbor. America was at war. The next September Bettie's boyfriend Billy Neal was drafted into the Army. He begged her to marry him. What if he got killed in the war? Didn't she owe it to him, now that he was off to fight for his country? "I was only nineteen and didn't want to get married for several years. I'll never know why I let him talk me into it, but on Saturday morning, February 18, 1943, I put on my black jersey dress and we rode the bus to Gallatin, a small town in Sumner County 30 miles from Nashville. We were married in the courthouse with two strangers as witnesses. Five minutes later when we were back on the bus, I asked myself, 'What have I done?'" She was

BETTIE PAGE

still a virgin.

Bettie and Billy lived briefly with his parents in Nashville. She never minded that Billy didn't go to college, but her pursuit of an education caused problems at home. Billy accused her of acting "high and mighty" because she attended college. His father also made snide comments about the "college girl." "It didn't bother me that Billy didn't go to college. But I wished I could have discussed literature with him since I'd been an avid reader all my life."

By 1944 all the men in Bettie Page's life were at war. Billy Neal went to boot camp in Mississippi. Oldest brother Billy Page served in the Army Corps of Engineers,

building bridges across Europe. Brother Jimmie was a gunner's mate on a destroyer in the Pacific, and youngest brother Jack was a cook on a destroyer escort. Then Billy Neal received orders to report to California pending assignment in the South Pacific.

Bettie received her B.A. from Peabody in June 1944. Four years at a teachers' college convinced her that she never wanted to teach school. "As part of my training, I had to teach English at a demonstration high

Above: Family gathering. Bettie in the only known photo with her father Roy (second from right).

school, but I found that I had a terrible time giving orders, and getting order, in that classroom. The boys made cat calls at me. They wouldn't be quiet at all. I was barely twenty-one and some of those students were eighteen and nineteen. I didn't like it at all, and I thought I would never teach again."

Disillusioned with teaching, Bettie tried to capitalize on her looks for the first time in her life. In 1944 the movie *Cover Girl*, starring Rita Hayworth, was released. To promote the film the studio staged "Cover Girl" beauty contests all over the United States. Bettie saw an ad in the local newspaper and submitted a headshot and a full-length photo. She placed second but nothing came of it.

As soon as she graduated, Bettie went to San Francisco to be with Billy. Within two weeks of her arrival, he shipped out to the

South Pacific. She settled in San Francisco, landing a job as a secretary for the sales manager of Enterprise Engine and Foundry Company. One day a visitor introduced himself as Art Grayson, president of Hollywood Commercial Motion Pictures,

Goldie and Bettie in 1941. "Goldie and I pretending to prepare for the *Ziegfeld Follies.* We were very brazen, posing right out in the front yard of Momma's house. We didn't care if the neighbors saw."

Christmas 1944 at the Parthenon in Nashville. "I loved that old rabbit fur coat! And that was my favorite red wool dress." Top: Jimmie, Bettie and Jack Page. Center: Goldie, Jack and Bettie. Bottom: Bettie with Jack. Opposite page: Bettie's first modeling composite, made in San Francisco in 1945.

and asked her if she would like to model for local newspaper ads. Grayson had several businesses, from a window-washing service to talent management to commercial production. He took many pictures of Bettie and sent some to 20th Century-Fox.

In 1945 the studio responded to the pictures of 22-year-old Bettie and invited her to Hollywood for a screen test. Bettie and Grayson made plans to fly down together, but he almost didn't make it because his wife suspected that he and Bettie were running away together. "Just as they were opening up the gate for us, Art's wife came running, hollering at her husband and grabbing him by the coattail. I kept telling her there was nothing between us. But he had to jump over the gate in order to get on the plane. He had never made a pass at me at all. But she just didn't believe it."

Bettie tested with the actor John Russell, who later starred in the television series *The Lawman*. The test didn't go well. Grayson annoyed the studio by leaving Bettie alone and going back to San Francisco immediately afterward. He was her agent, but he wasn't there to negotiate or intervene for her. Moreover, the studio and makeup team contrived to make Bettie look like Joan Crawford. She barely recognized herself; her sleek raven hair bunched out on the sides Crawford style, and she sported heavy black eyebrows and a dark, wide mouth almost twice its normal size. It was her own natural, fresh good looks that attracted their attention; it was a grotesque look-alike they saw on-screen. Bettie knew the test was awful, and she discovered later that the studio chiefs didn't like her Southern accent. But another incident perhaps contributed to the studio's rejection of her.

"An executive, one of the men I later learned was at the table deciding who would get the contracts and who wouldn't, had cornered me on the studio lot one day. He wanted me to go to dinner with him, but Art Grayson had told me not to go out with any of the men at the studio. I didn't like his looks and didn't want to go out with him anyhow. As he drove away, he said, 'You'll be sorry.' And I didn't get the contract. I'll never know, but he might have had something to do with it, because I wouldn't go to bed with him."

Depressed, Bettie returned to San Francisco. Hitherto athletic and health conscious, she gorged on doughnuts, ice cream and other sweets, and quickly gained 20 pounds. Ashamed of herself, she dieted and signed up for a $100 modeling course to get back into shape. She lost the weight quickly, but from the modeling course she gleaned little that would help her later in life. "I learned nothing from those people but how to walk with a book on top of my head."

Back in trim and optimistic again, Bettie entered another beauty

42

LANDLORD SAYS GIRLS BEAT HIM

A landlord vs. tenant battle which began with a broken wash basin and almost ended with a broken head – (the landlords) – wound up in Municipal Judge Daniel R. Shoemaker's court yesterday.

The complainant, who charged assault and battery, was landlord Joseph Pace, 52, of 1129 South Van Ness Avenue.

The defendants, who were given thirty-day suspended sentences and ordered to pay Pace $10 for broken glasses, were Bettie and Goldie Page, aged 22 and 21 respectively, of 1129 South Van Ness.

It all began, according to Pace, when he observed water flowing from the sisters' apartment Saturday night. He investigated, he told the court, and found that the basin had detached itself from the wall after Goldie stood in it to "shave her legs."

He told them his opinion on such matters and also requested back rent he claimed was owing. After a good sleep, he went back the next morning to tell them his opinions again.

Then, he declared, Bettie punched him in the eye, breaking his glasses, and Goldie smashed a milk bottle on his head.

The sisters, who pleaded not guilty, said Pace's version was wrong. Bettie said Pace socked her first and then rushed at her with fists upraised.

"He would have killed me if Goldie hadn't done something," she concluded, explaining Goldie's swing with the bottle.

Regarding the broken glasses, Goldie had this to say:

"He wasn't wearing glasses, and even if he had, I couldn't have broken them because I hit him on top of the head."

Goldie, Jack and Bettie in San Francisco, April 1946. "This was the heaviest I'd ever been, about 162 pounds! I took a modeling course to inspire me to lose weight."

contest she read about in the paper. The contest took place at the Paramount Theater in San Francisco, and was judged by sailors. Bettie wore tight black shorts and a white sweater, but she thought that a girl wearing a blue bikini and body makeup deserved first prize, a $100 war bond. Instead, Bettie says that as a lark the sailors gave first place to the girl wearing the least revealing outfit, an evening gown. "I just know they gave it to her because she wasn't wearing anything skimpy like the rest of us. The poor girl who should have won was so disappointed." Bettie came in second, receiving a $50 war bond as her prize.

She got her first modeling job for Geary Furriers, where she did secretarial work and modeled the coats for buyers. She still remembers the silky, sensuous feel of her favorite fur — ermine. "Better than mink!" she says. Then she got a better job at the Liliane Suit Company on Market Street, again combining modeling and secretarial work. Bettie and her sister Goldie shared a room in a boarding house on South Van Ness Avenue in the Mission District. The building was old and in poor condition. Bettie returned from work one night to find Goldie sitting at the bottom of the stairs crying her eyes out. Through her tears, she explained that as she shaved her legs in the bathroom, the sink fell off the wall. The landlord, whom Bettie describes as a "fiery little Italian guy," accused her of pulling the sink off the wall, cursed her and threatened to beat her up. Bettie was furious.

"I knocked on his door and told him

Above: Goldie, Jack and Bettie, San Francisco, 1946. Opposite page: Early portfolio shot of the aspiring starlet. "This was after my Fox screen test. My brother Jimmie sent me the grass skirt while he was in the Navy. My friend Guy Cross, a fabulous bodybuilder, took the photo in his San Francisco apartment. He taught me to waltz on ice skates at the Cliff House ice rink."

that he better never say another cuss word to my sister. The next morning he pounded on our door and as soon as I opened it, he flew in with fists flying right in my face. As soon as Goldie saw him attack me, she picked up an empty milk bottle and cracked him over the head, and blood was running down his face. I should have had him arrested for attacking me, but he had us arrested. Two detectives came out within an hour and hauled us down to the court-house. Because Goldie was underage, I'm the one who had to take the stand in the courtroom."

No one was in Municipal Judge Daniel Shoemaker's courtroom that day but a few photographers. Bettie took the blame for bashing Pace over the head, which landed her picture in the *San Francisco Examiner* on the morning of March 26, 1946. She paid a $10 fine for the glasses Pace claimed he wore and the charges were dropped. "I just hated that big old picture in the paper," she says, still annoyed with Pace. "I wasn't even the one who hit him!"

While Bettie and Goldie lived in San Francisco, Edna Page fell in love with Bill Darby, an Army sergeant sta-tioned outside Nashville. "She fell for him like a ton of bricks," Bettie says. Darby, a devout Catholic, married Edna and the two moved to Pittsburgh, where his mother and sisters — also devout Catholics — lived. Billy Page, just out of the Army, went to Pittsburgh to surprise the new Mrs. Darby. "I'd like to see my mother," he said to Darby's mother when she opened the door to their home. There was just one problem: Edna told the Darbys that she had never been married and had no children. She feared that a Catholic would never marry a divorced mother of six. "I don't know how she thought she could get away with such a cock-and-bull story like that, what with the six of us," Bettie exclaims. The couple never made peace with Edna's deceit and divorced in 1953.

Back in San Francisco, Art Grayson received a telegram from Warner Bros. inviting Bettie to Los Angeles for a second screentest. Bettie wanted another shot; she hoped that Warners' wouldn't attempt to transform her into a clone of an existing star. Then she received word that Billy Neal was on his way back from the South Pacific. She was not looking forward to his return. She resented that he had manipulated her into marriage. In San Francisco she was on her own for the first time in her life. She was 22, independent with her own job and apartment. Months before when she stopped using his last name, she knew it was over. She had already fallen for a sailor named Bob Mulligan, but she didn't have sex with him because she was married. Not wishing to write Billy a "Dear John" letter, she waited to tell him in person.

When Neal arrived in San Francisco in late April 1946, Bettie broke the news, and he was stunned, accusing her of sleeping with every sailor in town. They spent a month together trying to work things out, and Bettie got pregnant. But Billy didn't believe the baby was his. He claimed that an Army doctor told him he was sterile. "Boy, he flew into a rage. He said it wasn't his child, but of course it was, since I didn't have sex with anybody else. But Billy kept accusing me of sleeping around."

Bettie ignored the telegram from Warner Bros. and told Billy she would follow him back to Nashville. She still regrets not showing up for the screentest. "I'll never know what might have happened. But at the time, I was committed to my marriage." Billy went home and Bettie followed one month later. She moved into his parents' house with him, but they didn't get along. Billy was so jealous he refused to let her go to the movies or go skating with her own brother Jimmie. Shortly after she returned to Nashville, she miscarried. While she regrets not having children, she believes the child shouldn't have been born into that hostile atmosphere.

Bettie went to work for the Office of Price Administration and stayed with Billy at his parents' home until she saved enough money to leave. In 1947, deeply depressed about repeating the pattern of her parents' failed marriage, she left Nashville. Bettie had always wanted to see the Atlantic Ocean. She moved to Miami, though she had no job and didn't know a soul there.

Drifting
1947 to 1950

Above: Bettie,
Manhattan secretary.
At the Hudson River
with the New Jersey
Palisades in the
background, New
York, 1949.

Shortly after she arrived in Miami Beach, Bettie met a married couple in their 50s walking along the ocean. The husband ran a mahogany furniture business in Port-au-Prince, Haiti, and his wife owned a hat store in Miami. By the end of the conversation, he hired Bettie as a stenographer to accompany him to Haiti — his wife would stay behind and mind her store — to liquidate his business. The man agreed to pay her a salary plus plane fare and expenses.

Bettie loved Haiti; life in an exotic country intrigued her and in her free time she made Haitian friends and explored the terrain. She recalls riding a mule 3,000 feet up a mountain to the Citadelle la Ferrière, a fortress built by Henri Christophe, the former slave who became king of Haiti. Always interested in history, Bettie couldn't leave Haiti without visiting the landmark, even dismounting her donkey atop the steep promontory and crawling on her stomach to get a look over the side of the mountain.

During her four months in Haiti, Bettie had a "torrid love affair," but found out that the man was married. He lied about it, of course, but when she found out she refused to see him again. Before they broke up, however, the two had an unforgettable adventure, sneaking into the woods to watch the native people conduct a voodoo ritual. The pounding drumbeat and the men and women in masks dancing around a huge fire terrified her. The dancers appeared to be in a trance, preparing their bodies for possession by the *loas*

— deities wandering the earth.

When her job at the furniture company neared its conclusion, Bettie arranged to remain in the country working as a secretary to the U.S. Ambassador. She scrambled to get her papers and credentials from the United States in order, and looked forward to her new job which offered greater prestige and salary.

On Bettie's last day at the furniture business, the owner drove her from Cap-Haïtien to Port-au-Prince. After a couple of hours, he suggested that they stop and go for a walk in a swampy area dense with scrub trees. Once out of the car, he pounced on her without warning and tried to have sex with her. "I had worked for him for four months and he had never made a pass at me. He had been the perfect gentleman. When he grabbed me, I couldn't believe it. I started to cry like a baby, and managed to prevent him from actually penetrating me, but it was still a horrible experience," Bettie says.

Despite this ugly and humiliating incident, the resilient Bettie still had reasons to be optimistic. The man who had violated her trust was leaving the country and she would never have to see him again. In a few days she'd begin her new job at the embassy. But she changed her plans when Haitian students began to riot in the streets of Port-au-Prince. They threatened to kill all the Americans in Haiti because the Haitian president had failed to procure badly needed assistance from the United States. "I got panicky and frightened and took the next plane out of there," Bettie says. "But it was a shame! I was very much looking forward to that job."

Returning to Miami in the summer of 1947, Bettie didn't know what to do with her life. Then she met a well-known comedian named Jackie Whalen. They became

BETTIE PAGE

friends and he included her in his nightclub act, planting her in the audience and introducing her as Miss Tennessee. "Of course, I had never been Miss Tennessee, but for some reason, people believed it." If Bettie could impersonate a beauty queen, why couldn't she be an actress? She remembered how much she had loved acting in high school and college productions. If acting was her goal, New York would be her destination. Unfortunately, she was dead broke. Bettie told Whalen she wanted to go to New York and he gave her $50 to get there.

In the fall of 1947 Bettie arrived in Manhattan and got a secretarial job with the American Bread Company near Penn Station. Several days into her new job, as she strolled down Broadway in the evening looking into the windows of the shops, a tall, attractive young man started a conversation. He told her his name, and said that another couple, friends of his, were waiting for him on Eighth Avenue. They were all going dancing. Did she like to dance?

"I was a fiend for dancing, and he seemed so nice. So I told him yes, I'd like to go dancing." Bettie got into a car with him and the other couple. "Suddenly, we came to a red light, and two other guys jumped in. They introduced me to them, and I didn't think anything about it. Then we went farther on, and two more fellows got in the car. I still didn't think anything about it. I thought they were all going dancing too. We were crossing the Queensborough Bridge when all of a sudden it dawned on me that we weren't going dancing at all."

The men drove behind a school in Queens and the other girl went behind the building with her boyfriend. The four other men demanded that Bettie have sex with them. She told them she was menstruating and couldn't have sex, and they believed her. She thought she was safe, but they forced her to perform oral sex on each one of them. They even made her promise she would do the same thing again on Saturday night. "As soon as I got home, I called Billy

A Hudson River boat dock at 79th Street, with Riverside Drive penthouses in the background, October 1949. Bettie's note: "The photographer should be punched in the nose for moving the camera — this would have been a good picture."

we were walking down the street in Nashville and some boy I knew in school would cross the street to speak to me, he would accuse me of going out with him."

In November 1947 Bettie moved into the YWCA and filed for a divorce. "I was very unhappy about it. I still didn't want to be divorced like my parents, but I didn't see any way to make my marriage work." After she had the papers served, Billy cornered her outside the YWCA and threatened to hurt her if she went ahead with the divorce.

long distance in Nashville and told him that I was coming home. I didn't tell him what had happened to me, but I was just frightened to death of New York. That was one of the worst things that ever happened to me. I've never told it to my family, though. I just kept it to myself."

Bettie hurried home to Nashville and got a job working for the L&N Railroad in the Coach, Paint and Tank Shop near Centennial Park. Open to the possibility of a reconciliation, she moved in with Billy, still her legal husband. After the experiences she had suffered as a single woman, the security of marriage promised a safe haven. Unfortunately, Billy's jealousy hadn't diminished during their separation. Bettie's close relationship with her own brothers threatened him. "Jimmie was heartbroken when Billy wouldn't let me go anywhere with him — my own brother. I got sick of his flying into rages over nothing. If

Despite her horrible experience in Queens, Bettie summoned up her courage and went back to New York. She landed a job as secretary to a real estate developer, Joseph Sussman, and an insurance broker, J. H. Lehds, who shared offices in the Eastern Airlines Building at Rockefeller Plaza. She enjoyed the job and it paid well. She began to feel at home in the city, delighting in her little apartment on 78th Street between Columbus and Amsterdam, for which she paid a mere six dollars a week. The house was run by an Irish woman, Mrs. Murphy, who took a liking to the girl from Nashville. She treated her more like a niece than a tenant. She worried about a girl alone in the city.

But Billy Neal followed Bettie to New York and appeared at her door one day threatening to kill himself if she didn't let him in. When a neighbor heard the noise and intervened, Billy cut the man's face with a knife. Bettie felt miserable about the wounding of her friend, a man in his 50s who was only trying to help her. She called Billy's father and begged him to order his son home.

When Billy left New York, Bettie continued to work at Rockefeller Plaza. One day in early January 1948 she was typing at her desk when she felt someone staring at her.

She looked up and saw a handsome, dark-haired man. He smiled and returned at the end of the day to introduce himself. He was Carlos Garcia Arrese, a student from Lima, Peru, studying engineering at New York University. Bettie worked on the ninth floor and the Peruvian Embassy happened to be next door. "I think I fell in love with him right then and there," Bettie says. "By the time I got home, my landlady said he had been calling for an hour or so."

Carlos and Bettie began dating. An

Fall 1949, New York. After surviving a brutal assault and being disappointed in love, a pensive Bettie walked along a desolate New York lake, wondering what the future held. She didn't know that the life that lay ahead would immortalize her. In less than a year she was discovered on a Coney Island beach, and her life would change forever.

excellent dancer, he taught her the mambo, rhumba and samba. They danced all night long and also indulged Bettie's other passion — going to the movies. "I was also making mad love with him," Bettie says.

One evening in April 1948 Bettie was at Carlos's apartment when someone started banging on the door. A woman screamed, "Carlos, open the door! I know you're in there with her!" Needless to say, it was his wife — the beautiful blonde whose picture Carlos carried in his wallet. Another married man! On their first date he had told Bettie that the woman and the little boy in the photograph were his sister and nephew. In truth, his wife and little son had been living in Albany with her in-laws while he attended school in the city. "I tried to tell her that I didn't know he was married, but she called me every name in the book including 'homewrecker.' I left there feeling lower than a snake."

Carlos continued to call Bettie, but she refused to see him. He tried the patience of Mrs. Murphy because Bettie lived on the fifth floor of the brownstone and had to be called down to

the phone every time he called. Finally she agreed to see him. In tears he said he loved her, but he knew she wouldn't have seen him if he had confessed he was married. Bettie still loved him, but the betrayal stung her and she ended the affair. Still, it was difficult to let go, and she didn't forget Carlos for a long time. "I had a hard time getting over him. I guess if ever I was in love with a man, it was Carlos."

For the rest of 1948 and 1949 Bettie continued working at Rockefeller Plaza. By late 1949 she longed for the beaches, warm weather and palm trees of Florida. She closed up her apartment in early 1950 and went to visit her sister Joyce in Coral Gables, Florida. When she arrived, Billy Neal began to write to her from Atlanta, where he was working in a shoe store.

Neal's letters, filled with love and remorse, begged her to try again. He apologized for being a bad husband and urged her to visit him. Guilty over her failed marriage, Bettie went to Atlanta, but the visit lasted less than a month. After a final argument Bettie went to the bus station and asked how far the $16 in her pocket would take her. For $14.50 she bought a ticket to Washington, D.C., arriving with less than two dollars in her pocket. The Travelers' Aid Society found her a room in a large boardinghouse and a job as secretary to an insurance agent. The agent was just starting his business and didn't have many clients, so he and his new secretary often took the afternoon off to play golf. The athletic Bettie was a natural on the course. "There was nothing else between us," she says.

Opposite page, top: Bettie and one of her young friends, Spring Valley, New York, September 1950. Opposite page, bottom, and above: Edna and Bettie Page on Bettie's front lawn. Washington, D.C., Spring 1950.

Labor Day outing with one of the children of the family Bettie lived with after Greenbush Summer Theater. September 1950, Spring Valley, New York. Above: "Me and one of my 'boyfriends,' Gary White, age five, and his puppies. Aren't they cute? The dogs, I mean." Top: Downtown Spring Valley. Left: At monument dedicated to servicemen, Memorial Park, Spring Valley. Bettie Page, the all-American girl next door, just days before she moved to Manhattan, and less than one month before her discovery as America's greatest pin-up.

"It was the easiest job I ever had."

In the spring of 1950 Bettie read an ad in the paper for apprenticeships at the Greenbush Summer Theater near Nyack, New York. Though she'd done nothing to pursue a career, acting was still in the back of her mind. She was accepted and in early summer left Washington and her leisurely job for Nyack. At Greenbush she performed the duties of a young theater apprentice: scene painting, props and stage management. She landed the small role of Mabel, a floozy in the comedy *Three Men on a Horse*.

At the end of the season Bettie got a job in nearby Spring Valley, New York, working for a lawyer. Boarding in the home of a family with four little boys and a bunch of puppies, she enjoyed hiking in the woods to a lake, where she dove and swam. She also dated a local boy named Tommy who had a motorcycle. Bettie remembers riding through the countryside with him: "I loved the wind on my face." Tommy used to sing "Good Night Irene" to Bettie when he dropped her off. After about a month, with a little money saved, and encouraged by her happy experience at Greenbush, Bettie returned to New York.

She was 27 years old. Single and with no prospects, Bettie seemed headed for a life typical for a woman of her time. Another secretarial job. A second marriage, perhaps. A family and a quiet life. In September 1950 Bettie Page landed in New York City, unaware that the life that lay ahead would immortalize her.

Top: Bettie at the Nashville airport in front of an old stagger-wing plane. "I remember getting sick as a dog when we hit air pockets and the plane swooped down suddenly. I had a hard time keeping my lunch down!" Below: Bettie on Columbus Avenue in Coral Gables, Florida, while visiting her sister Joyce early in 1950, before she moved to Washington, D. C. in the spring and New York City that fall.

PART TWO

*Accidental
Legend*

Bettie in her glory days. On the beach in New York, surrounded by camera club photographers. Their shadows fall across the sand and her body.

The Camera Clubs

She presents an image which transcends all time.
—Art Amsie

I n New York Bettie got another secretarial job and found an apartment on West 46th Street between Fifth and Sixth Avenues. "I saw an ad in the paper for a fourth floor walk-up next to the Wentworth Hotel. I painted and decorated the whole thing — made the drapes, covered the couch and two chairs in the living room, tiled the bathroom and the kitchenette and had fun doing it. It was seedy looking when I moved in, but it was only forty-six dollars and twenty-nine cents a month. Imagine!" Bettie kept an aquarium of angel fish and guppies that she called her "miniature friends."

Bettie was in New York again, but she was no closer to an acting career than before. She was an anonymous secretary, working all week and taking long lonely walks on weekends dreaming of a more glamorous life. It was during a walk on a deserted beach at Coney Island on a chilly October afternoon in 1950 that a chance encounter changed her life and made her a legend. Bettie remembers it vividly. "I was wearing a sweater and slacks. The beach was empty, except for one guy doing his exercises — a very well-built black fellow, nice looking. I sat down and watched him for about a half an hour until he finished, and then he came over and asked me if I had ever done any photographic modeling. His name was Jerry Tibbs. He was a New York City policeman, but his hobby was photographing models. He gave me his card, and offered to make up a portfolio for me free of charge."

That Monday Bettie went to Tibbs's Brooklyn studio, where he took many pin-up style pictures of her. "Those were my first pin-up photos. He had several bikinis which I put on,

Above: Bettie and camera club ace Art Amsie.

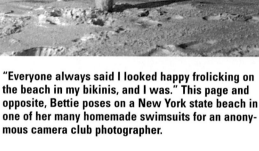

"Everyone always said I looked happy frolicking on the beach in my bikinis, and I was." This page and opposite, Bettie poses on a New York state beach in one of her many homemade swimsuits for an anonymous camera club photographer.

but I didn't like what he did with my breasts! He had me stuff Kleenex inside the bikini. I wasn't skinny at all in those days. I didn't need the Kleenex, but I didn't say anything to him. Jerry published my first cover on a Harlem newsprint magazine. He used pictures of me on four or five covers of that little magazine. He was a very good photographer."

Through trial and error, Tibbs tried to improve Bettie's look. He enhanced her cleavage. He retouched her face. Then he painted in long eyelashes. Finally he discovered the secret: He told her to cut her hair in bangs. "Jerry said I had a very high protruding forehead, and that I'd look good with bangs. I've been wearing them ever since." Bettie shot with Tibbs many times and remembers him with fondness. "All the time I was in New York, he'd phone me every now and then to see how I was, and to tell me about the models he was photographing.

He started it all."

Tibbs introduced Bettie to Cass Carr, a black Jamaican musician, bandleader and photographer who ran several camera

phere." She remembers that the clubs often included women photographers; it wasn't rare to find one or two in each group.

Carr paid Bettie $10 an hour to pose in

3-D slides shot by an anonymous camera club member, circa 1954-55.

clubs. She shot with Carr's group, the Lens Art Camera Club, at the Harlem YMCA on West 132nd Street until Carr moved midtown, where he started the Concorde Camera Circle at DeLogue Studios, 118 West 47th Street, just a few minutes' walk from Bettie's apartment.

Carr organized the camera club sessions and charged the other photographers a fee. On weekends the clubs took Bettie and two or three other models to Westchester County in upstate New York, to the Headley Farm along Route 80 in New Jersey or to Jones Beach on Fire Island to spend the day picnicking and shooting outdoors. Bettie enjoyed the outdoor sessions more than the studio work, which she complained didn't have enough variety. "Cass had a nice studio, but he used the same old background all the time. There wasn't much change."

At a camera club shoot, whether in the studio or outdoors, the photographers formed a semicircle around one model and shot her simultaneously. Bettie describes the sessions as having a "homey atmos-

the studio and $25 for the outdoor shoots. Soon she exceeded her secretarial salary of $40 per week, top pay for clerical work. Modeling freed her from the tedium of a desk job. While she always found good jobs, Bettie was bored with office work. Though an excellent secretary, she was also a natural bohemian and a free spirit with an advanced case of wanderlust — a personality much more suited to the flexible hours and creative environment of the modeling scene.

The camera clubs challenged the conservative social mores of the 1950s. Because the shutterbugs took photographs for their personal use and not for publication or sending through the mail, the clubs weren't bound by the same laws that censored nudity in magazines. Nudity appeared only in "art" magazines, or the "health" magazines like *Modern Sunbathing, Sunshine and Health* and *Sunbathing and Hygiene* — all thinly disguised excuses to enjoy the sight of naked women. The clubs, on the other hand, encouraged nude modeling. Taking off her bikini for the first time, Bettie did some of her most daring posing for them.

The anonym
tographer w
many 3-D sli
Bettie also t
fantasy sequ
ing her behi
frame to cor
own paintin

conservative Southern city. In these years prior to the Civil Rights Movement, how did a young woman from Tennessee manage to transcend the pervasive racial prejudice of the time?

Bettie says that her time in Haiti raised her consciousness. "I was a big baseball fan when I was very young. My idol was Burt Haas, a first baseman for the Nashville Vols, and I would go to see him whenever I could. When I was about thirteen, I was walking along the street by the Capitol building picking up cigarette packages to find baseball cards. Two black girls came along,

"From the first time I posed nude, I wasn't embarrassed or anything," she says nonchalantly. She says it never occurred to her to be shy in front of the camera. "I never thought it was terrible to be in the nude. After all, God created man and woman totally nude and put them in the garden. If they hadn't turned against Him and disobeyed Him, they might have remained in the nude all their lives." Bettie says that she even toyed with the idea of joining a nudist colony, but never actually paid a visit to one. "It just seemed natural to me. I was always very happy walking around the house in the nude. When the camera clubs would shoot outdoors in New Jersey, I would go traipsing around in the woods in the buff. I was never self-conscious about it."

Also, the Concorde Camera Club Circle was a racially mixed group. Bettie wasn't the only white model posing nude for black photographers — a social taboo even in liberal New York City. But Bettie was from a

Opposite: Bettie in 3-D regards herself in 2-D with amusement.

This page: More 3-D fantasies.

Above: A camera club photographer shot this nude of Bettie in a studio session. **Opposite:** This set of 4 x 5s was sold from "under the counter" at newsstands or by mail order in the late 1950s. Ads in magazines for the set read, "We've got pictures...the kind men like."

py about that, and so bitter."

Cass Carr's Concorde Camera Circle became Bettie's regular gig. At one of these sessions she modeled for the famous Weegee, the photojournalist nicknamed after a Ouija Board because he always showed up first on the scene of an event. As Bettie became more well known, Carr hired her as "the draw" along with a few amateur models. According to several of the club members, when Bettie modeled she attracted as many as 25 photographers, but on days she was absent, the crowd was as small as 10.

"She was the Michael Jordan of modeling. The best that ever was; the best there'll ever be," declares Art Amsie, a retired electronics engineer and renowned historian of American pin-up art. Amsie was a member of the Concorde Camera Circle during the latter 1950s until he started his own club, Associated Photographers.

From 1956 through 1957, Amsie shot 3-D color slides of Bettie. Three-dimensional photography is accomplished by a stereo camera, which takes two photographs simultaneously at slightly different angles. It required a precise style of posing to which Bettie adapted readily. Amsie's recipe for a good pin-up is "Clothes, Pose and Expression." Amsie preferred photographing Bettie in bikinis or lingerie, not nude. "With the pin-up, you must pay attention to hands, arms, legs, torso, fingers, neck, face. If one thing is wrong, you have nothing. And sometimes, in correcting one little thing, another aspect goes awry. The model must find the perfect pose and then hold it, looking perfectly natural and unstilted.

"Bettie and I were simpatico," he says. Even if he gave her an unusual pose, she executed it easily. "I loved going outside with her and shooting her against a tree, or out in a cornfield, or on the beach, splashing around in the water. One cold spring

grabbed my pictures out of my hand and started pushing me around. That angered me so, and I thought I didn't care for black people after that. But then I went to Haiti, and met so many nice black people and mulattos. That experience took all of the prejudice out of me."

Bettie sympathized with her friend Jerry Tibbs and his wife. "Jerry was married to a Jewish girl he loved very much, but back then there was so much prejudice, he couldn't even take her to a restaurant. They just wouldn't let him in. He was very unhap-

Arthur Fellig, the infamous photojournalist known as "Weegee," shot Bettie during several camera club sessions. According to some camera club members, he loved to joke with her, and jumped into a bathtub full of water with her while she posed.

day when we were on Fire Island, there were three little amateur girls huddled under a blanket while Bettie was in the water splashing around. The water was probably 60 degrees at that time of year. She must have been freezing her tushy off, but when you look at the photos, there is no indication." If he was short of ideas, she suggested things. "You could talk to her conceptually. Bettie was intelligent. I would throw a couple of phrases at her, and she would say, 'Ah, I know.' And she would do it." If Bettie didn't like his ideas, she'd joke with him to make him realize they wouldn't work. When Amsie suggested she bring garter belts to the next beach shoot, Bettie replied, "Good idea, Art. Garter belts and sand. Yes, that should work well."

When Cass Carr offered free sessions to photographers willing to drive a group to the location, Amsie took advantage of the situation, not only saving five dollars but commandeering Bettie to sit in the front seat beside him in the first car of the camera club motorcade. "What am I, stupid? I put three photographers in the back seat and Bettie in the front with me." Amsie loved having her sitting beside him in his car, and delighted in imagining that the three guys in the back were "licking their chops." But there was nothing flagrantly sexual about Bettie when she wasn't in front of the camera. "Our conversations were about everyday, simple things. She was just real people." Amsie says that even when he told her how much he loved her lingerie shots, Bettie laughed, "Oh Art, you and your lingerie!"

On location sometimes Amsie wandered to another model, thinking he'd shot enough of Bettie. "But guess what? I'd spend so much time posing them, and then I'd look through the viewfinder and say 'no good.' After a roll, I'd always find myself

coming back to Bettie because she was the best. She had grace."

In the early 1950s Addison Yeaman, Jr., an Economics major at Yale University, came to New York on weekends to go to the theater and to visit his godfather. Upon arrival, he would telephone Carr's studio to find out if a studio session was scheduled that weekend. If Bettie Page was modeling, he made every effort to get to the studio. "If the model were anyone other than Bettie, I'd make an effort, but if my plans were thwarted, I wasn't disappointed," he recalls. On about ten or fifteen weekends, until he graduated in June 1953, Yeaman paid his five dollars to Carr and, along with other shutterbugs, photographed Bettie. "Bettie turned on in front of the camera," says Yeaman. "I suspect she was a true exhibitionist. She seemed to enjoy modeling as much as she enjoyed making a living at it. The Bettie Page smile and the Bettie Page twinkle in her eye went a long way."

Don Whitney, an optical engineer in Massachusetts, had been a photography enthusiast since the age of nine. In the 1950s, he traveled to New York on business and his photographic equipment traveled with him. During one trip in 1957, he rented studio space to photograph a figure model. He telephoned a studio on West 56th Street and requested an hour of time plus a model. He was thrilled to learn that his model would be the famous pin-up, Bettie Page. On the evening of the appointment, he went to the studio where the woman who ran the place entrusted him with a key and told him to lock up when he finished. He introduced himself to Bettie, and took twenty slides.

"She was a charming person and a fabulous model," he says. "Out of the twenty nudes I took with a hand-held 35mm Kodak Retina III-C, amazingly, all came out fine.

She could strike any pose you wanted. Her expressions and body positions were always perfect and tasteful. She didn't even blink her eyes." Whitney was struck by the fact that Bettie worked hard to please him, though he was an out-of-town amateur. "I got the impression she was there to do the very best she could, though I suspect it was relatively effortless. She was just a natural." Art Amsie echoes this observation. "Bettie put out the best she could whether she was posing for a star photographer or Joe Rumpelstiltskin," he declares. "She gave her best all the time. That's a very significant feature of her career. I never took one bad photograph of her." Bettie corroborates their testimony. She never discriminated against photographers no matter what their level of talent or notoriety; nor did she consider what she was being paid. "I just did the best I could every time I was in front of the camera. That was my responsibility."

Buck Henry, the writer and actor, was also present on some of the camera club adventures. Henry dated one of the models and accompanied her on several of Bettie's shoots. He recalls how the amateur photographers and "professional perverts, voyeurs," as he perceived them, paid to follow the models around with their cameras while they stripped, dressed and posed. "I just knew when I saw Bettie that she was better than anyone else," Henry testifies. He believes that while the photographers were in awe of Bettie, some of them didn't even have film in their cameras. "Hey, film was expensive," agrees Art Amsie. "Many of these guys just wanted to look at pretty girls." While this may be true, many of the photographers did take pictures, judging by the hundreds and hundreds of photos that survive.

In this era of repressed sexual desire, access to beautiful nude women was part of

Bettie with camera club shutterbug and pal Art Amsie in 1956-57. "I should have married her," Amsie says wistfully today. "I still want to."

This page and opposite: Photography buff Don Whitney shot Bettie during one session in 1957 when he rented studio space in New York and hired a model by the hour. Whitney developed the color film in his basement, because professional labs wouldn't develop nude photographs.

tele consists of sexually frustrated, introverted men who'd rather look than do." Bettie had one bad experience with the camera clubs. She went to a party with several members who encouraged her to take a drink or two. Bettie, who never drank, got drunk quickly and posed nude in ways more explicit than she'd previously done. She barely remembers the evening. Later, the police confiscated the photos when one of the men tried to sell them. Two officers brought the pictures to Bettie's front door,

the lure of the camera clubs. While voyeuristic curiosity must have motivated some camera club members, their behavior didn't reflect it. "Even this tacky group treated her like a demi-goddess," Buck Henry observed. Addison Yeaman recalls that Bettie's conduct, and that of the photographers, was always "quite proper" in the studio — no more and no less than if she were modeling in an art school. "She talked and joked with the photographers, but she always changed in the dressing room. While she struck new poses, no one took pictures that inadvertently showed more than she wanted." Like the other photographers, Yeaman had no contact with Bettie outside the studio. "As a young and callow college student, I certainly wanted to, but I didn't." Still, the camera clubs did have a certain unsavory reputation. An issue of *Vice-Squad* magazine characterized the camera club members as sexual shysters posing as photographers, and the models as innocents "sucked into a dangerous game by some shrewd, fast-talking operators. The weirdest experiences are everyday occurrences of the camera club cuties because their clien-

calling them pornographic and demanding to know their source. By today's standards, they could hardly be called so; she was nude, but no sex act was depicted or implied. But Bettie heard a rumor that the photographer served a few months in prison for taking the pictures.

Because many of the members were

BETTIE PAGE

amateurs, and some were simply voyeurs, the camera clubs produced a body of work that varies widely in quality. Much of it was out of focus and poorly composed, but some of the photographs from more serious hobbyists like Amsie were high quality and rivaled the professional pin-up photographers of the day. Whatever the caliber, as a body of work it is an important archive of an era. Sadly, because of the clandestine nature of sexuality and the prevailing attitude toward nudity in the Fifties, many of the photographs have been destroyed, while others remain closeted. Don Whitney recalls, "It wasn't socially acceptable at the time. The mere fact that they couldn't be processed commercially indicates that." Whitney had to learn to process color film in his cellar because commercial labs wouldn't process nudes, and photographs showing pubic hair couldn't be mailed. "It was ridiculous because these shots were extremely tasteful. Bettie wouldn't have done anything that could be considered 'pornographic' even if I asked her, which I didn't."

Don Whitney and Addison Yeaman are sophisticated men who have no shame or embarrassment about their involvement in the camera clubs 40 years ago. "Yes, my wife knows all about Bettie," Whitney says, amused that some would keep it a secret. But his photos were almost lost for good. He forgot what he did with the slides until his hot-water heater burst and he had to move several boxes in his basement to replace it. There, in a box unopened for more than 30 years, were the pictures.

Opposite: Christmas in kitschland. The ultimate 1950s fantasia by the anonymous 3-D photographer.
Below: Bettie on the farm, by Art Amsie.

Addison Yeaman recalls that he threw away negatives of Bettie Page over the years when he thought a wife or girlfriend wouldn't want them around. Only a few rolls from his many sessions with Bettie survive.

Bettie confirms that the camera clubs engaged in a form of sexual expression that was ahead of the time. "It's a wonder I didn't get arrested," she exclaims, and then remembers that during one of these sessions she did have a brush with the law. She was arrested for indecent exposure in a small community in upstate New York. The shutter-bugs picked a spot to shoot not far off the highway, where passing drivers saw the models, who were topless or in bikinis. An outraged citizen called the sheriff, and Bettie and the entire group were taken in squad cars to the local courthouse and held there for five hours. Bettie and the others refused to plead guilty to any charges. When she insisted that she was not indecent and that the group was a legitimate camera club from New York City, the judge finally fined each person five dollars, and made them agree to never return to their town. Not all the shutterbugs were as comfortable with their activities as Bettie Page. To this day, remnants of shame exist. Some camera club members still refuse to show their work and prefer not to be identified for fear of offending the women in their lives or of jeopardizing their status in their communities or in their business lives. Many of the photographs from the camera club adventures still await discovery, hidden for decades in the closets, basements and dresser drawers of the men — and the occasional women — who took them.

This page, opposite and following two pages: 1956-57. Photographs by Art Amsie: "I didn't even bother shooting Bettie indoors. She loved posing outside. She put out more when she was outdoors."

This page and opposite: Fire Island, April 1956. Bettie makes merry in freezing cold water while Art Amsie shoots. Though it doesn't show in the pictures, it was a very chilly day, and the other camera club models huddled under a blanket while Bettie posed for Art.

BETTIE PAGE

A classic Art Amsie photo of Bettie on the beach. Bettie made all her own bikinis for the camera club beach sessions. "I remember dreaming up designs, and then shopping and shopping until I found just the right fabrics and trim. I loved sewing my own bathing costumes."

Bettie complained about the boring backdrops at Cass Carr's studio, which is why she preferred to shoot outdoors. Despite the mundane settings, she never stopped trying new poses.

Bettie poses for Art Amsie in a home-made bathing suit.

Bettie on a New York beach by an anonymous camera club photographer.

For changes of scenery, the camera clubs sometimes convened at members' apartments. Left: In the early 1970s, artist Robert Blue based one of his large oils of Bettie on this photo.

96　　BETTIE PAGE

"That was one of my wildest bikini designs," Bettie recalls. This page: "I remember shooting against that old net, and trying to think of new things to do."

A rare, never-before published "strip" sequence, shot by an anonymous camera club photographer, possibly shot at a studio, but more likely a member's apartment. These photos were taken early in Bettie's modeling career, the skirt and blouse remnants of her days as a secretary. The fake cardboard fireplace and flames typified the low-budget ambiance of camera club shoots.

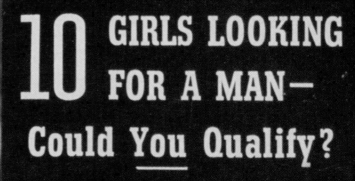

SHOW

A HILLMAN PUBLICATION

DECEMBER

10¢

10 GIRLS LOOKING FOR A MAN — Could You Qualify?

also

RITA MORENO:
Pocket-Size A-Bomb

BOLD Cover Girl

Few women can match Betty Page for sheer ability to enjoy life. But then, few could equal Miss Page in any of the qualifications she displays so well for Bold's April cover, and this portfolio. Her instinctive, uninhibited grace is reinforced by sparkling teeth, midnight-black

When Robert Harrison featured Bettie by name in his men's magazines, her pin-up career took off. She posed for dozens of digest-size magazines like this one.

The Men's Magazines

Within a few months Bettie Page became the most popular camera club model in New York, but outside club circles she remained unknown. The camera club photos were ephemeral, taken for the photographers' personal enjoyment, and they were never published. And Bettie didn't try to capitalize on her growing popularity. "I never took pictures around to the studios, professional photographers or the magazines. I was never very ambitious in those years. I was still brooding over my unhappy marriage and the divorce."

But even with her doing nothing to advance her career, it moved ahead on its own. In early 1951 a camera club photographer tried to sell some pictures of her to the leading publisher of men's magazines, Robert Harrison. Harrison loved what he saw and hired Bettie to pose for all his publications: *Wink, Titter, Beauty Parade* and *Eyeful*. Capitalizing on the World War II fascination with the pin-up, Harrison's magazines were considered scandalous at the time, but none featured a trace of nudity; most of his layouts showed models acting out spoof scenarios, comic strip style, complete with joke captions. Bettie posed for all of them, appearing as everything from a scantily clad maid to a "sailor" in a bikini. In "Gal and a Gorilla," she zipped around town in the arms of her "constant escort," Gus — a man in a very silly ape costume. Sometimes a more "serious" Bettie wore heels and a monocle — a glimpse of the dark angel to come. In *Thy Neighbor's Wife*, Gay Talese observed that Robert Harrison's magazines portrayed sex as bizarre behavior, and "his high-heeled heroines with whips and frowning faces were, in the best Puritan tradition, offering punishment for pleasure."

They're in the NAVY Now!

These Goofy Gobs Should Be in the Whacks!

THERE'S somethin' about a sailor, fellers, particularly sea sigh-wrens like this. It seems that Cassie and Dolly decided to help Uncle Sam, so they joined the Navy, which is sure a funny place for a coupla whacks like these to land! Anyway, this is what happens when chorus girls go gob. Up anchor, gang!

This was Bettie's public debut as a pin-up queen. Through the magazines, hundreds of thousands of men learned the name Bettie Page. But the early Bettie was not at the height of her power. In most of the spreads she wears on her face a perpetual gasp of surprise. She clowns, goofs and teases for the camera, but the confident seductress has not yet emerged.

Bettie remembers with amusement Harrison's obsession with his models' cleavage. "I always resented it because he insisted that all the models be taped in the breast, and it was uncomfortable. From the side view your breasts looked terrible. It wasn't flattering at all. Only front views were good. Besides, I don't think I needed the help."

Bettie was, in fact, less voluptuous than some of the competition. Unlike June Wilkinson, Mamie Van Doren, Tempest Storm, Blaze Starr, Jayne Mansfield and others, Bettie didn't fit the mold of the stereotypical big-breasted pin-up. Though she was womanly, she was sleek, firm and well exercised — an athletic American girl. This was no accident; Bettie worked hard to maintain her body. She ate only fresh, natural foods, a diet she follows to this day. She didn't drink alcohol, never smoked and never experimented with drugs. She embraced a wholesome lifestyle long before it became a national obsession. "I was very much involved in the health club at the Central Park Hotel on Sixth Avenue. I would go at least three times a week and work out in the gym using the machines. I would also go swimming a lot. They had a great big heated pool with a waterfall at one end of it. I loved it there."

Also, Bettie was a brunette in a universe of blondes — most of them fake. Bob Schultz, pin-up expert and dean of Bettie Page collectors, stresses the point. "Bettie could have gotten away with being a blonde — her skin was fair and her eyes were blue. But she remained herself — the natural girl-next-door. That set her apart from the crowd and is a very important reason why she endured."

Once Bettie appeared in Harrison's magazines, every men's magazine in the country clamored to publish her photos. She was a star, but only in the pin-up world. Unlike today, there was no crossover from sex symbol to high fashion; that world was closed to her. Even the mainstream sex symbol of the day, Marilyn Monroe, was considered too vulgar for the cover of *Vogue* or *Harper's Bazaar*. The high-fashion magazines scorned sensual covers with wanton-looking models.

While fashion models posed for a specific magazine, Bettie rarely knew where the photographs taken of her would appear. Like Harrison, other publishers owned many magazines, and often they commissioned photos before they knew how they would use them. Nor did Bettie go out of her way to look for her pictures on the newsstands. Unless a friend, photographer or another model showed them to her, she never saw them.

In 1951 Harrison, a flamboyant promoter, had Bettie appear at the Beaux Arts Ball at the Waldorf Astoria. "I was wearing two telephone dials on the breasts with a suggestion box right across the front, and a pair of fishnet tights up to the waist. That's all I had on." Harrison proposed the costume himself. Bettie won first place for her efforts, and the title Queen of the Ball. "I won a big set of Revere kitchenware with all kinds of nice pots and pans. And let me tell you, I was happy to have it." Bettie won the title "Miss Pin-Up Girl of the World" for 1955, and placed first in the "Queen of the Food Industry" contest, also

Harrison's first publication was *Beauty Parade: Glorifying the American Girl.* By the early 1950s, he published eight men's magazines.

GAL and a gorilla

Listen, you big ape! Do you help the girl friend shop like this?

Gus the gorilla is handy around the house! Well, who could refuse Bettie?

At busy corners, an ape is a nice help to a helpless babe! Nice armful, Gus!

BETTIE PAGE, page one chorus chick, is in the headlines again, boys! Beautiful Bettie has a tame gorilla as her constant escort! It may sound crazy, but Bettie ain't bothered by mashers, Bub!

GALS THINK MEN ARE BEASTS, AND THIS DOLL THINKS A GORILLA IS A SAFER BOYFRIEND, YOU WOLF!

He's a good skate when Baby decides to take the air, and tough if you whistle at her!

Bettie's a knockout, 'n Gus the gorilla plays dead when they spar! We would too, Gus!

When the soprano reaches for a high note, what if she lost her skirt? We're waitin' too!

WHAT YOU'D LIKE TO SEE ON TV

Those panel shows! If only they'd get so mad that the show would end in a brawl!

TIRED T. V. SHOWS DRIVIN' YOU NUTS? WOULDN'T IT

YOU a video vidiot? The same old shows slowly drivin' you off your rocker? Wouldn't it be fun if some of these crises happened in the middle of a program? If you agree, you're a devil, but just the same, we don't blame you! Here's proof of just how much sport it'd be, pal!

Some day, while a doctor's comparin' cigarettes, some cutie will cough — we hope!

And on *You Bet Your Shirt*, we live for the day a gal really does lose hers, eh?

IN IF THESE THINGS HAPPENED ON VIDEO, YOU RASCAL!

held at the Waldorf Astoria.

Men across America adored Bettie Page but, strangely, her family refused to recognize her success. Knowing full well that she was a pin-up star, they never said a word about it. When neighbors back home asked what Bettie was doing, the stock answer was "working in New York." On her many visits home, the family never discussed Bettie's career, even though Goldie visited her in New York and posed a couple of times with her for the camera clubs.

Yet Bettie says she remained close to her mother during the modeling years. They didn't write many letters, but once Edna divorced Darby and was back in Nashville, Bettie sent money home, often telephoned her for long chats and spent holidays in Nashville with her family.

While Edna refused to discuss Bettie's career, she collected her daughter's photographs secretly. "Years later, after I had stopped modeling, I went home one time when Momma wasn't in the house. I found in her closet a big stack of magazines. She had all of my old pin-ups from *Wink*, *Flirt* and all the rest." During Bettie's entire career, Edna never told her that she had seen one picture of her in a magazine. "She never

said a thing to me about it. But all those years she saved them in the back of the closet." Bettie believes that Edna collected the magazines while working as a cashier at Union Station in Nashville, where there was a big newsstand near her counter.

Back in New York, Bettie brought to her profession another talent learned years ago at the community center in Nashville. She was a crackerjack seamstress who began making her own bikinis and other costumes for the photo sessions. In her free time, she dreamed up designs and shopped for fabric and trim to execute her creations. Others noticed her flair. A married couple claiming to be photographers hired Bettie for several hours and asked her to pose in all of her bikinis and costumes. As with any photo session, she didn't know how they would use the pictures. Later she was shocked when the photos from that session appeared in magazine ads. The couple started a bikini manufacturing business by copying Bettie's designs. Shameless, they used photos of Bettie in her own outfits to advertise their products. "I never did anything about it, but they sold those things to promote bootleg products."

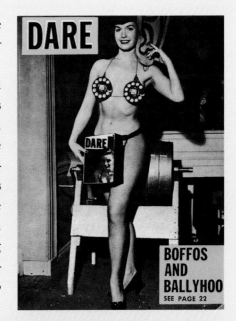

ABOVE: PRIZE WINNERS ARE BETTIE PAGE, J. ROLAND SALA, CHRIS JORGENSEN, LYNN CONNORS. IN FRONT, LUDWIG BARTSH. RIGHT: HELLO,

BOFFOS AND
BALLYHOO
22

Bettie with other "Best Costume" winners at the 1951 Beaux Arts Ball at the Waldorf Astoria. Robert Harrison designed her costume.

APRIL 1956

BOLD

15¢

BETTY PAGE PIN-UP PORTFOLIO

HOLLYWOOD SEX GOES RUGGED

Betty Page

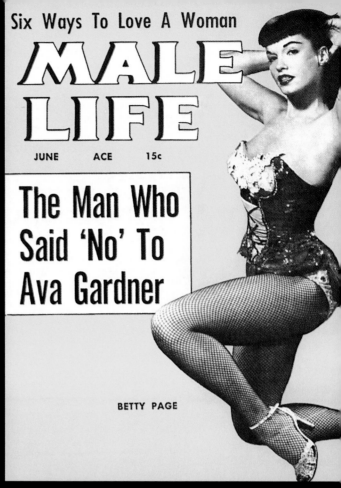

Six Ways To Love A Woman

MALE LIFE

JUNE   ACE   15¢

The Man Who Said 'No' To Ava Gardner

BETTY PAGE

BLACK NYLONS
SEMI-ANNUAL
VOL. 2   ISSUE NO. 2

AND

HIGH HEELS

The Magazine for Artists and Photographers

APRIL 25¢

Foto-rama

PDC

THE FORBIDDEN SEX-RITES OF THE TROPICS

THE PLACE THEY CALL "PIG-ALLEY"

BETTY PAGE

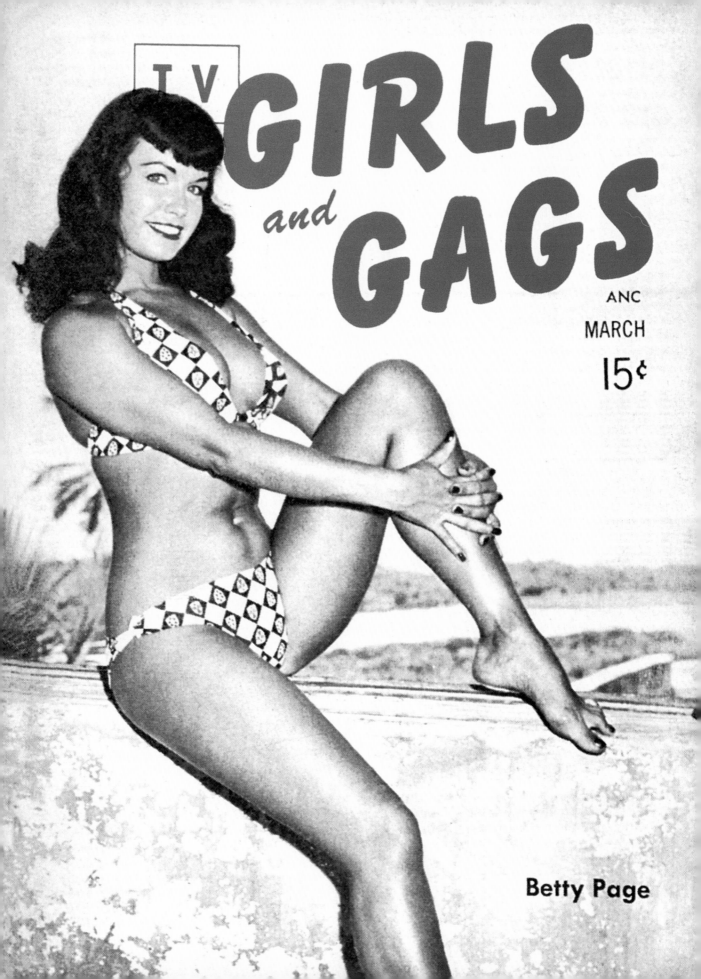

TV GIRLS and GAGS

ANC MARCH

15¢

Betty Page

Bettie continued to pose for Harrison's and other pin-up publications until she quit modeling in 1957. Though this type of magazine survived until the early 1960s, their heyday was over. The new sexual ideology of Hugh Hefner's more overt, daring and slick *Playboy* made them obsolete. While Harrison's magazines didn't make it into the liberated new era, Bettie Page did. She was the centerspread for *Playboy*'s January 1955 holiday issue. Holding a Christmas ornament and wearing nothing but a Santa Claus cap, she winked at the camera.

From a contemporary perspective, it's difficult to understand the effect *Playboy* had on a culture where sexual desire was judged an unsavory part of human nature, better left closeted. In *Thy Neighbor's Wife*, Gay Talese noted that in the 1950s, the media characterized sexual activity as "smut," which gave editors the opportunity to satisfy their readers' prurient interests while simultaneously expressing disapproval. Prior to *Playboy*, even men's magazines like *Pose*, *Peep Show*, *Bold* and *Dare* presented sex as unwholesome — either as vice or scandal. They juxtaposed sensational stories of crime against pictures of semi-nude women. Though cultural pioneer Hugh Hefner advocated sex as a normal and inevitable part of life, and researcher Alfred Kinsey's report demonstrated that American men and women engaged in a wide variety of sexual activities, acceptance of sexual desire was hardly part of mainstream ideology.

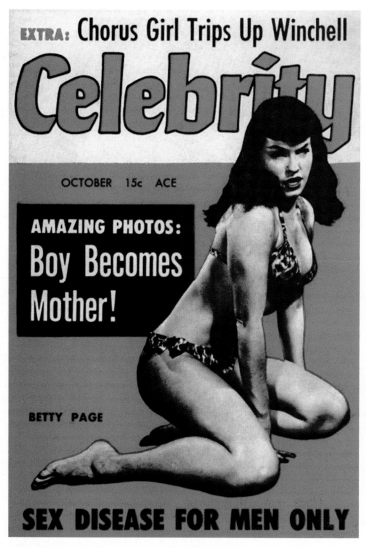

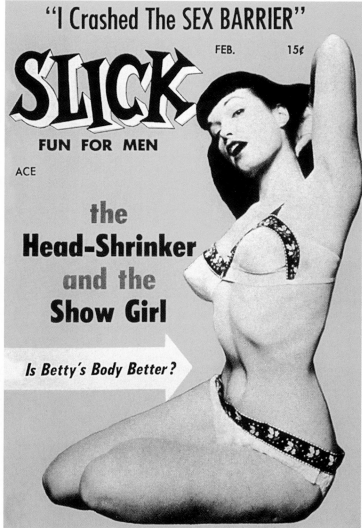

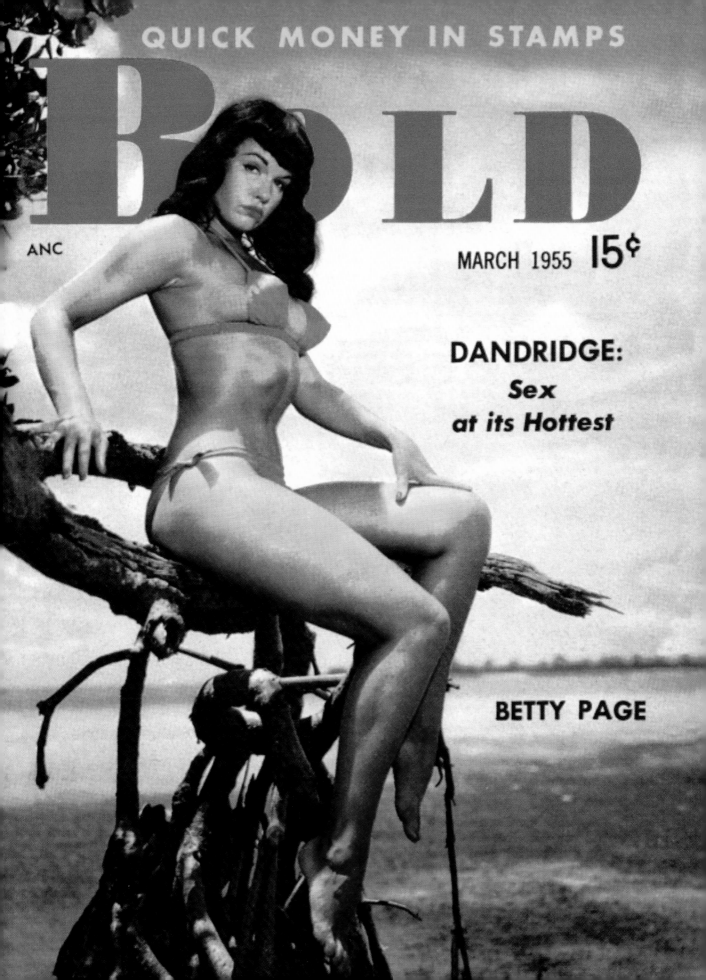

QUICK MONEY IN STAMPS

BOLD

ANC

MARCH 1955   15¢

DANDRIDGE:
*Sex
at its Hottest*

BETTY PAGE

Dream-Lined!

PASS the sleepin' pills, gents, 'cause here's Bettie Page, a dream-lined doll from St. Paul.

Just to help your dream-in' along, have some facts about Bettie. She's only 20, 5'5½" tall, jet black hair, sultry brown eyes, 36" bust, 24" waist, 36½" hips, 8½" ankles, 12½" calves, and 19½ lovely inches round her thighs!

STRIP the BANK

A QUIZ, JOE. YOU GET $1 FOR EACH "YES" ANSWER!

Bikini manufacturers, posing as photographers hiring a model, spent a session photographing Bettie in the bikinis and other costumes she designed. They copied every one and sold them for years, unabashedly using Bettie's own pictures in their ads.

"I'M SORT OF THE IN-
TELLECTUAL TYPE, YOU
KNOW, GLASSES 'N ALL!"

Posed by
BETTIE PAGE

America's Most Beautiful Cover Girl

New York, 1953. *See* magazine "Cover Girl" beauty contest. "I came in seventh, but I can't believe I placed at all. The night before, my sister Goldie and I went out on the town with two fellows. We galavanted all night long, and the next day I had horrible circles under my eyes. I wore an old white bathing suit I had made that really didn't flatter me at all. Elaine Stewart won that contest. She went on to have a small part as a starlet—which she was—in the Kirk Douglas and Lana Turner movie, *The Bad and the Beautiful*."

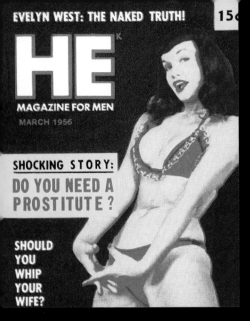

EVELYN WEST: THE NAKED TRUTH!

15¢

HE
MAGAZINE FOR MEN

MARCH 1956

SHOCKING STORY:

DO YOU NEED A PROSTITUTE?

SHOULD YOU WHIP YOUR WIFE?

GAZE
GAZE

TURN TO FUN WHEN YOUR WORK IS DONE... READ

GAZE!

OCT 25¢

CARTOONS, JOKES, PHOTO-FUN!

"I TOLD MOMMA YOU NEVER PUT A HAND ON ME... MOMMA WANTS TO KNOW IF YOU'RE SERIOUS!"

"A recent survey shows that fifty percent of the modern girls smoke a pack a day," says Betty Paige, "while the other fifty percent are satisfied with a puff!"

ALL-AMERICAN MUCHACHARAMA! MAN'S GAGS!

A HUMORAMA MAGAZINE

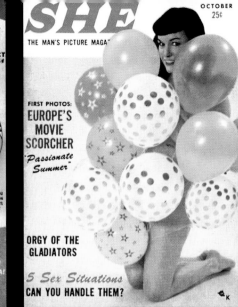

SHE

OCTOBER 25¢

THE MAN'S PICTURE MAGAZINE

FIRST PHOTOS: EUROPE'S MOVIE SCORCHER *"Passionate Summer"*

ORGY OF THE GLADIATORS

5 Sex Situations
CAN YOU HANDLE THEM?

BLACK NYLONS
Vol. 1, Issue No. 1

AND

HIGH HEELS

The Magazine for Artists and Photographers

VOLUME 2
ISSUE 1
$1.00

BOLD

ADULTS ONLY

GIRLS!

SEE CENTER SPREAD FOR 10 LIFE SIZE PINUPS OF BEAUTIFUL GIRLS IN 4 COLORS

ANNIE'S BOSOM OF NATURE!

OLD FLAMES BURN BRIGHT!

WAXING AND WINNING!

STARE

STARE

APRIL 35¢

EXCITING & LIVELY PICTURE PLEASURE!

HOW I BECAME A SUCCESSFUL MADEL!

MASKED 'N MARVELOUS!

GRETA THYSSEN!

MARLA ENGLISH!

BETTY PAGE!

MORALE BOOSTERS! MAIDEN, U.S.A.! DRAMARAMA!

FRIENDS ARE ALWAYS DOING THINGS FOR ME!

LAUNCHING A HEAVENLY BODY!

GIGGLES & WIGGLES

plus a galarray of lusty & robust photo varieties!

JOKER

The Only Magazine With JEsT Propulsion!

JOKER

AUG.

IN GAGS WE TRUST

GAGS FOR STAGS! CARTOON GEMS!

SIGHFUL EYEFUL:

BETTY PAGE!

"A case like this comes up once in a great wile!"

PIN-UPS! GALARAMA!

A HUMORAMA MAGAZINE

"I was told so much about the birds and the bees that I'm always up a tree when it comes to men!"

RUGGED

Entertainment for Real Men

APRIL 35¢ PGC

Why your girl friends are nuts about
ELVIS PRESLEY,
JIMMY DEAN,
PAT BOONE and
BILL HALEY
by Frank Kane

MAN'S
MAGAZINE

ADULTERY IS MY BUSINESS

Iron Duke of Pro Football

CONFESSIONS OF A MEDIUM

HOW TO SHOOT YOUR WIFE

Exclusive! OUR FIRST WAR WITH RUSSIA!

FEB. 25c

TAB

THE POCKET
PICTURE MAGAZINE

HOW WE LICKED THE
TEEN AGE
SIN-CLUBS

∎

Raiding with
the Foreign
Legion!

∎

THE GIRL WHO
MADE GOOD
BEING BAD

∎

BETTE PAIGE

PAGE
is the
RAGE

MORE ➤

When the men's magazines published Bettie's pictures, they quoted her, and printed stories about her activities, and likes and dislikes, though she never gave them an interview.

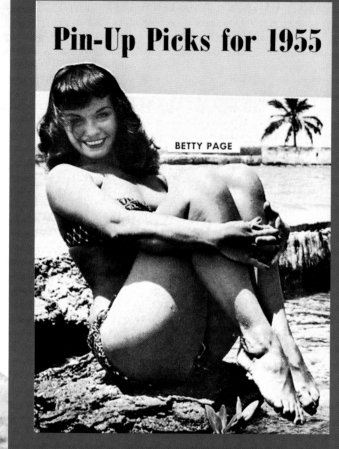

Pin-Up Picks for 1955

BETTY PAGE

BOLD COVER GIRL

Not content with day modeling alone, Betty at night has a small role in a New York play. No one's found the explanation for Betty's endless reserves of energy. But some guess such a power-source could only be the sun, which she absorbs in enviable quantities each day.

FRONT PAGE NEWS

Model Bettie Page, who's graced the covers of so many magazines, has recently been named "The Girl with the Perfect Figure," which certainly makes good news.

AUG.
SUNBATHING
FOR **HEALTH MAGAZINE**

50¢

THE NUDIST PICTURE MAGAZINE

FEBRUARY 1955 50c

modern
Sunbathing

hygiene

PEOPLE WHO
CAN'T BE
NUDISTS

Las Vegas
Strip...

AMERICA'S BIGGEST NUDIST CAMP

THE NUDIST PICTURE NEWS

APRIL 1956 50c

modern
Sunbathing

FAMOUS
PHYSICAL CULTURIST
says "Nudism gave me
a second chance!"

DIARY OF A YOUNG GIRL

BETTIE PAGE
NUDE BUT NOT
NAKED

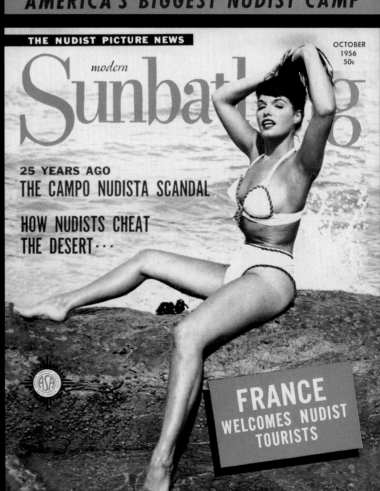

THE NUDIST PICTURE NEWS

OCTOBER
1956
50c

modern
Sunbathing

25 YEARS AGO
THE CAMPO NUDISTA SCANDAL

HOW NUDISTS CHEAT
THE DESERT···

FRANCE
WELCOMES NUDIST
TOURISTS

MARCH

SUNBATHING
FOR
HEALTH MAGAZINE

50¢

Carnival

JUNE 15¢

A HILLMAN PUBLICATION

7 NEW WAYS TO INCREASE YOUR SEX LIFE

A Talent Scout Tells

WILL GIRLS DO ANYTHING TO GET ON TV?

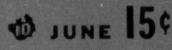

THE NAKED TRUTH
NOVEMBER 1954

BARE

¢25

WHITE GIRLS RECRUITED FOR Singapore's DENS!

HAREM BEAUTIES UNVEILED

HOW GIRLS CHEAT MEN!

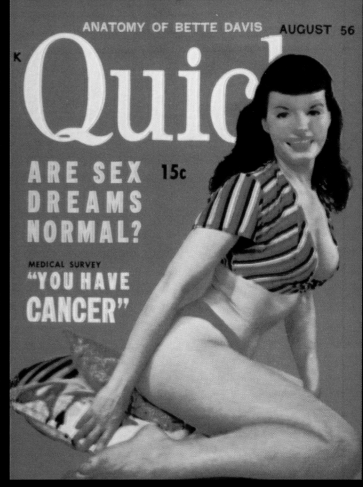

ANATOMY OF BETTE DAVIS   AUGUST 56

K

Quick

15c

ARE SEX DREAMS NORMAL?

MEDICAL SURVEY
"YOU HAVE CANCER"

JEST

JEST

CARTOONS—JOKES—GAGS!

Grand ole' Country Humor!

for all our Country Cousins!

NOV. 25¢

A HUMORAMA MAGAZINE

JAKE

"The Boss had to lay her off, so we're taking a weekly collection to keep her around!"

BETTY PAGE says some men like to think they are part wolf they act more like w—

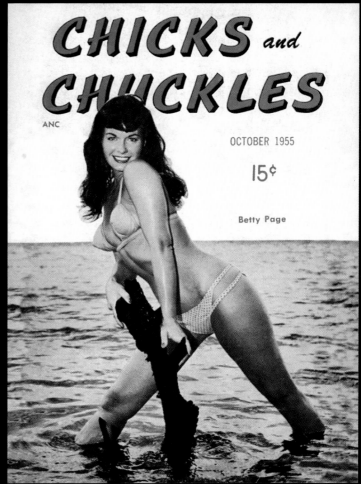

CHICKS and CHUCKLES

ANC

OCTOBER 1955

15¢

Betty Page

SIX PAGES OF BETTY PAIGE!

(see inside)

BETTY PAIGE:

JUST WAITING TO GIVE HIM THE GATE!

POINT

Betty Page has made a fabulous success of modeling. The reasons are obvious.

EASY ON THE AHS: BETTY PAGE!

COMEDY

MAY 25¢

PLENTY OF FUN

FAST AND LIVELY ENTERTAINMENT

JAKE

"Will you scram?! You're making me promise things which I could never make good!"

QUIPS BY PIPS!

FUN ON THE RUN!

PICK - ME - UPS!

"There's talk that the dress designers are again considering raising their sights. All I can say," comments BETTY PAGE, "is that they had better do it calf-fully!"

A HUMORAMA MAGAZINE

SPECIAL FIGURE SALON

MAY 1955 50c

ART Photography

MAGAZINE
PHOTOGRAPHY:
IT'S MURDER!

MAKE YOUR CAMERA PAY OFF!

ONE MAN'S OPINION:
"PHOTOGRAPHY IS NOT AN ART!"

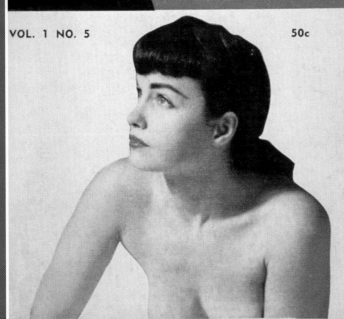

Occasionally, Bettie worked as a figure model for artists. She also posed for magazines catering specifically to "artists," though they were usually designed to appeal to the voyeur.

Bettie was one of the few models who warranted publications devoted solely to her. In these cover-to-cover photo books, her fans were treated to rare nude or semi-nude photos. More candid than the Harrison publications or the digest magazines and slicker than the others, these pictures were shot in the photographer's home or on a set made to resemble an apartment. They sold for the outrageous price of 50 cents to one dollar at a time when magazines were 25 cents.

Bettie's newfound fame as a magazine pin-up enabled her to once and for all leave secretarial work behind. "I never had any problem getting a job, back in those days. But I didn't like sitting at a typewriter all day. It was boring! After a few months in an office I'd want to quit and go travel. I was too much of a wanderer to be an office worker. That's why modeling suited me so."

Charmand's
CATALOGUE OF FASHION

1956 BIKINI-SIZE EDITION   **25¢**

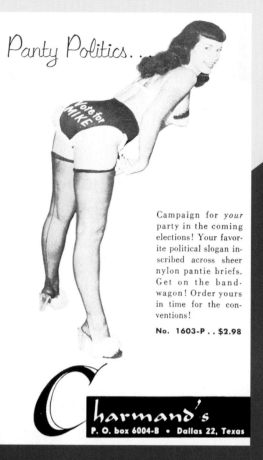

Panty Politics...

Campaign for *your* party in the coming elections! Your favorite political slogan inscribed across sheer nylon pantie briefs. Get on the bandwagon! Order yours in time for the conventions!

No. 1603-P . . $2.98

Charmand's
P. O. box 6004-B • Dallas 22, Texas

**Above: This catalogue featured Bettie's own designs, but she didn't know it when she posed for these pictures.
Below: A typical men's magazine spread.**

Sound Effects by BETTY PAGE!

HIS face was plain—she did not care—
His hair was slightly long,
And though his clothes were out of style,
He gave her heart a song!

10

SHE pressed his likeness to her cheek
And held it fondly there,
And then she kissed it ardently,
Her love thus to declare.

11

SHE looked at Ben, adoring him,
She tingled with a thrill;
She loved B. Franklin's portrait on
That hundred-dollar bill!

12

IDAHO VICE TRAP

SIR!

annual

★

WHY SHELLEY WON'T POSE IN THE NUDE

★

THE HEYDAY OF *Prostitution*

★

NUDISM EXPLAINED

★

Bettie Page

HALO

Best Musical Comedy Songs longplay

THE BEST MUSICAL COMEDY SONGS

The Broadway Singers and Orchestra

I Could Have Danced All Night
Standing on the Corner
(Excerpt from Act I, Scene 2,
of "The Most Happy Fella")
Summertime
June Is Busting Out All Over
Some Enchanted Evening
A Wand'ring Minstrel
Donkey Serenade
People Will Say We're in Love
Make Believe
Deep in My Heart, Dear
They Say It's Wonderful
You're the Top

high fidelity

In addition to the countless men's magazines, Bettie's image soon graced the covers of record albums and pocketbooks, calendars and postcards, even playing cards and matchbooks.

At the height of her fame, she even posed as a "Femme Fatale" on these two covers for the popular Ellery Queen digest.

TUXEDO
BOOK
120

60c
LN

Their time was running out
and with reckless abandon
they spent their remaining
hours in a wanton splurge
of carnal lusts!!

SEX MERRY-GO-ROUND

JACK MOORE

A TUXEDO ORIGINAL

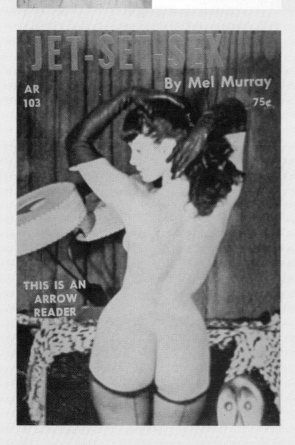

JET-SET SEX

AR
103

By Mel Murray

75¢

THIS IS AN
ARROW
READER

BETTIE PAGE

WOW! WE ALLIGATORS
DO HAVE FUN
IN NEW ORLEANS!

5♥

1955	FEBRUARY				1955	
SUN	MON	TUE	WED	THU	FRI	SAT
«»	«»	1	2	3	4	5
6	7	8	9	10	11	12
13	14	15	16	17	18	19
20	21	22	23	24	25	26
27	28	«»	«»	«»	«»	«»

VUE

AMERICA'S PHOTO DIGEST

HOW TO SPOT A BEAUTY

APR. 25c

PASSION WITH
A PROWL CAR

SECRET FOTOS
*HOUNDS OF
HELL*

BUY A WIFE
FOR $80

Those Sexy
Swedes

BETTIE PAGE

● ● Bouncing Betty Page, one of the country's top pin-up models, recently found herself involved in a heated controversy with some Greenwich Village friends over the relative merits of the female body, ancient and modern. Who had more to offer? A typical young damsel in Ancient Greece, or a typical young dame in Modern America?

You can guess which side of the argument Betty was on. After looking at her picture, you might even agree with her. We certainly wouldn't blame you if you did. But, to prove her point, Betty agreed to model opposite a plaster cast of a statue of ancient vintage, borrowed for

Betty's a success as a pin-up model. Anyone wonder why?

Here Betty invites comparison with old master. Select one

the occasion from a New York art school. The burning question was, unfortunately, never finally settled, and must make up his own mind.

But whatever his mind, it isn't hard for modern man to note the obvious charms of Miss Page. Florida born, she came to New York two years ago to crack into the theater, and has been working ever since. ●

Richard Merkin, a New York artist and writer, and a long-time Bettie Page fan with an impressive collection of her photos and memorabilia, remembers vividly the secretive atmosphere surrounding sex in the era of his boyhood and his burgeoning sexual curiosity. "If you didn't live through the Fifties, you can't imagine just how controlled it all was at that time. One of the amazing things about this period is that it's so unavailable," Merkin says. "People were furtive in the 1950s."

By the mid Fifties the men's magazines sold at the newsstands in Times Square were full of pictures of Bettie Page, but none of them were explicit nudes. Young men like Buck Henry and Richard Merkin wanted the real stuff. They scoffed at the occasional "tasteful" nude available in Playboy, the art journals and the sunbathing magazines, and haunted the stands for illicit camera club photos sold under the table. Henry remembers loitering around the stands, skimming the girlie magazines, waiting for the

Centerfold for an issue of *Satan* magazine, a 1950's men's magazine. Bettie appeared on the cover of this issue with a dapper, tuxedoed devil.
Above: A 1950s men's magazine compared Bettie's body to classical sculpture.

Mink, jewels and Betty Page—what a combination. Even SATAN, that old reprobate, is tempted by the scene!

ARE YOU DRAWLING?

Laura holds twelve titles, including "Miss Nashville" and "Miss Picnic."

Back in Tennessee, Laura won a number of beauty contests by unanimous vote.

Pardon her Southern accent, but Laura Kavanaugh recently arrived in N. Y. from Nashville. She's been in summer stock, sung in a niteclub and this is her first modeling job. Actually the main accent is on her loveliness, for men from any part of the U.S. can appreciate this refreshing bit of Southern exposure.

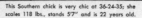

This Southern chick is very chic at 36-24-35; she scales 118 lbs., stands 5'7" and is 22 years old.

Teevy has yet to use Laura, a natural for such a medium. She has lots of radio experience, though.

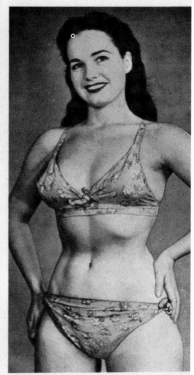

Beauty runs in her family. Her cousin's model Betty Paige.

12

13

cigar-smoking clerk giving him the fish-eye to discern his true interests. At a newsstand on the corner of 48th and Seventh Avenue, Henry purchased several provocative 4X5 nude photos of Bettie. He paid the high price of thirteen dollars, "a lot of money back then for someone who was living by stealing from the A&P and doing a play here and there."

Merkin recalls a newsstand on 42nd Street. The man behind the counter had "a face like scrambled eggs," and kept an eye on the gentlemen customers, whom Merkin remembers as "respectable business types wearing their 'Madison Avenue crash helmets' and carrying attaché cases." Gauging his client's true interests, the clerk reached under the counter at just the right moment and dropped a stack of photos of nude women in front of Merkin. "I was just a boy, and I was staring at these things. But the Madison Avenue guy, in his lockjaw voice, picked up the photos and studied them in amazement. 'Wow!' he said. 'These things are rare!' As if he's looking at Gutenberg Bibles. And the guy with the scrambled-egg face laughed and said, 'Yeah, they're rare. They're rare and they're raw.'"

Merkin says that men were desperate for the nudes they couldn't buy in the men's magazines — so desperate that the women in the forbidden photos ranged in looks from true beauties like Bettie Page to frumps. "If a woman disrobed, someone would buy the picture."

Above: *Frolic* magazine discovered early photos of a bangless Bettie and exploited them as shots of her visiting Southern cousin, Laura Kavanaugh.

Opposite: Bettie as one of the first centerfolds for a new men's magazine called *Playboy.* She played Santa in the January 1955 holiday issue. Forty years later, Playboy has published the centerfold as a limited edition photograph signed by Hugh M. Hefner and Bettie Page.

Dark Angel
Fetish, Bondage and Method Acting

Bettie Page was Manhattan's favorite camera club girl and on her way to becoming queen of the men's magazines. If she had achieved that and nothing more, she might be remembered today as just another glamour girl of a bygone era — recalled with nostalgic fondness along with Diane Webber, Irish McCalla, June Wilkinson, Betty Brosmer and the others. But then she did something that transcended her time and made her a legend. She transformed herself from all-American girl into a dark angel of hidden desire. In late 1951 or early 1952 — concurrently with her camera club and men's magazine modeling — Bettie began modeling for Irving Klaw, New York's pin-up and bondage king. In the late 1940s and 1950s, Irving's business, Movie Star News, was a factory of pin-up art and photography. Originally, Irving and his sister Paula bought publicity photos from the Hollywood studios, but their customers wanted more. They decided to make their own. Setting up a photography studio on the second floor of their building on 14th Street, they shot the photos upstairs, had them processed by an outside lab and sold them downstairs in their store and through mail-order catalogues.

In the late 1940s, a diminutive, soft-spoken bondage enthusiast known as "Little John" asked the Klaws to take custom photographs for him. John held a high-profile federal job; to this day Paula refuses to disclose his identity. To communicate his desires, John showed Paula "damsels in distress" photos — women tied to railroad tracks, or dangling perilously from ropes out of airplanes. John struck a deal with the Klaws: He agreed to pay the model's fee, furnish the costumes and ropes and buy the photographs. The Klaws got to keep the negatives and the right to sell prints to other customers.

A relationship developed and John and Paula became collaborators. At his suggestion, Paula stockpiled a collection of fetish costumes and props. He advised her on what to purchase and demanded the highest quality accessories for his shoots — fancy silk and satin lingerie, expensive black leather gloves, handmade high heels. In special cases he provided the goods himself — custom-made leather and rubber bondage gear imported from Europe. From John, Paula learned even more about the fetish world: the intricate rope techniques practiced by bondage

enthusiasts. Paula tied and trussed all the models, and did not allow the others in the studio to touch them.

Once word got out, other fetishists approached the Klaws to take photos for them. Paula, a vital, savvy woman who still runs Movie Star News, recalls the parade of accoutrements that came through the Klaw studios. "A leather enthusiast would bring in leather outfits, and someone who liked chains would bring in a chain outfit. Then the rubber people would bring in something custom-made in Italy. Then there were guys who brought me the shoes with the extremely high heels they had made by an Italian bootmaker. We had the spanking fanatics, and those who liked to see girls fighting. We had the garter-belt customers, the bare-feet customers — all the fetishists."

Neither Bettie nor Paula remembers who introduced them, except that he was a camera-club photographer. "Bettie posed for the camera clubs, and one of my customers had taken pictures of her," Paula recollects. "He thought she was a great model, so he brought her to the store on Fourteenth Street. Once she started working for us, we could tell right away by the sales that our customers liked her, so we used her at every shoot. Besides, she was so great to work with."

Almost every week, and often on Saturdays, Bettie modeled for the Klaws until the end of her career in 1957. Irving directed, and hired a few men to take the photographs. Soon Paula learned from the freelancers how to take pictures. "They handed me a camera, and said 'This is what you do.' But my shots were beautiful. My favorite camera was the Speed-graphic 4 x 5." Paula took many of the famous photos of Bettie, though she never sought credit. Only in recent years has she disclosed the information.

Irving supervised while Paula and two other photographers shot the models. The group worked all day, breaking only for lunch when the Klaws brought food in for the crew. Like all modeling, posing for the Klaws was hard work. Hair, makeup and styling preceded hours of standing, posing and holding unnatural positions. Bettie was a photographer's dream; she worked without complaint, tried new poses, proposed ideas and costumes and

Bettie models the jacket worn by the softball team that Irving Klaw sponsored.

Above: Resplendent in a black leather dress and fetish accessories. Opposite page: Bettie, laughing with Irving Klaw in a candid photo shot after Irving put his foot through the prop steps. "Irving was a wonderful man. Though I was often late for our sessions — sometimes as much as an hour — he never said a word about it. He never got angry with me."

"Irving scolded me only one time," says Art Amsie, harkening back to the days when he would spend hours picking through the lingerie photos. "I asked him, 'What are all these pictures of people tied up?' And he shushed me. He said, 'They're my best customers. They spend a lot of money!'"

"Irving really liked his work," Bettie says, "and so did Paula. Irving didn't talk much. He watched everything, and gave instructions now and then." Bettie says that Paula's presence made the models feel safe. "I was the only one who would go into the dressing room," Paula confirms. "The photographers would have died to go in there and talk to the girls, but I wouldn't allow it."

Bettie and the Klaws became friends. After a day's work, Paula and Irving often treated Bettie to dinner. "We only took Bettie," Paula recollects. "She was like a member of the family at this point." According to Paula, Bettie deserved the special treatment. "She was a super model. The best: very easy to work with, diplomatic, personality plus." Besides that, she never complained during the long shoots. The group's favorite spot was The Morocco, where Paula's husband, Jack Kramer, would join them. They always escorted Bettie home, and made sure she got upstairs safely. "We had a big sister/little sister relationship," Paula says.

In October 1953 Bettie appeared in *Striporama*, a feature-length burlesque film produced by theater owner Martin Lewis. Bettie remembers sitting around for days during the shoot while she waited for her scene. The film, starring Lili St. Cyr, featured Bettie taking a bubble bath in a white bikini, a sequence billed as "the most daring bath scene ever filmed." Inspired by the success of *Striporama*, one year later Irving Klaw produced *Varietease*, another feature-length film starring St. Cyr, with Bettie in a dance number. In 1955 he went on to present *Teaserama*,

presented a fresh face for the camera even when she was tired.

In spite of the hard work — and the kinky subject matter — the Klaws' studio had a casual atmosphere. Irving was a shrewd businessman who knew how to capitalize on a good thing and how far to go within the limits of the law. But he was also jovial, good-natured and respectful of the models — a far cry from the cliché of a man exploiting women's sexuality for profit.

Still photographs taken on the sets of Bettie's 8mm and 16mm dance loops. Though her fans covet these short films for the playfulness and joy she exhibits, Bettie declares that she was far from a professional dancer, and had to "wing it" in each loop with no musical accompaniment.

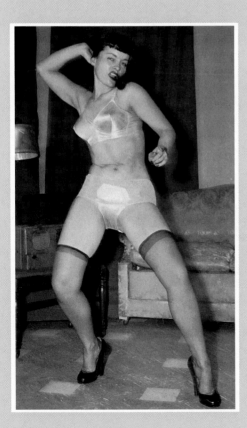

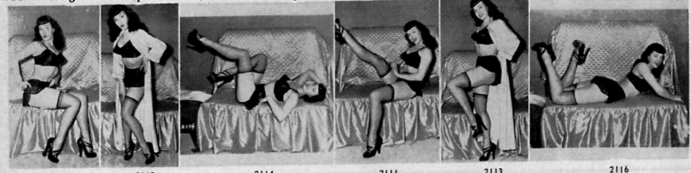
starring Tempest Storm, the impressively voluptuous burlesque stripper with flowing, flaming red hair. Bettie wears a French maid costume and "attends" to Tempest, playing a younger apprentice to the more sophisticated star. At the end of the 10-minute segment, Bettie mocks Tempest by imitating her primping. In punishment for her audacity, Tempest pulls Bettie's hair. Later Bettie appears in a succession of outfits introducing the other acts — burlesque dancers and comedians — with placards.

The Klaws also produced 8mm and 16mm short films — five to eight minutes long — called loops. Approximately 50 of them featured Bettie, and Paula shot many of them. No more than a social and ballroom dancer, Bettie appeared in several loops as a solo dancer. With no musical accompaniment she had to "wing it," dancing in costume to the beat of music in her head. "I had taken tap dancing for seven or eight months at a little studio on Seventh Avenue. And I had taken six months of ballet when I was in San Francisco in 1944. But that was it," she says. The phonograph and radio that appear in

some of the films were simply mute props. In one film, she actually danced over to the radio to turn on some music. "But it wasn't on," she laughs. "I had to wiggle around by myself, doing anything that came to mind. There was never any music."

Each dance film had a different title: *Tambourine Dance, Spanish Shawl Dance by Betty, Flirtatious Dance by Betty.* "But they were all the same thing!" she exclaims. "I was terrible!" In the bondage-oriented loops, Bettie played both dominant and submissive roles, victimizing or being victimized by Roz Greenwood, among others. The fetish loops include *Hobbled in Kid Leather Harness,* in which "bad" Bettie wears a harness and is spanked by Patricia Midblane, and *French Garter Fight,* with Bettie and Jackie Lens doing battle over a garter. In *Betty Gets Bound and Kidnapped,* two women drug "good" Bettie, strip her to her bra and panties and tie her up. Perhaps the most bizarre of the loops is *Betty's Clown Dance, Parts I & II.* In risqué lingerie, she cuddles, hugs and dances with a stuffed clown. In a strange Oedipal fantasy, Bettie treats the toy clown in alternately maternal and erotic ways.

Though the Klaws rarely shot outside the studio, they took several models to the home of a client in upstate New York who offered his beautiful house on large, manicured grounds as a location. In one film loop shot that day, Bettie and Roz

Greenwood tied up another girl, walked her outside, put her in the trunk of a car and slammed the lid. In another, they tied a girl to a tree. "We just made the scenes up as we went along on that day," Paula recalls. On her own without specific direction from a client, Paula performed her duties well. "I got the award that day — best tie-er." In this relaxed atmosphere, the client enjoyed a special treat; he made drinks for the Klaws and the models at his own bar after the shoot.

Bettie's exuberance in these short films is astonishing. In the bondage loops, her playfulness and animated style undercut the severe sexual implications. In the burlesque films, she one-upped the professional dancers who preened for the camera with studied coyness. Bettie was

unschooled, but far sexier in her uninhibited enthusiasm. Always, she gave the impression in front of the camera that she was a real girl — accessible and genuine. What was her secret? "I would often think of the camera as a man," she says.

To the Klaws, bondage was strictly business; to Bettie Page it was fun. She claims she wasn't a

Opposite page: Irving and Bettie discuss a shot during a break. "For years it was rumored that Irving and I were involved, but that was ridiculous. We were like family. Irving had nothing but a professional relationship with his models."

Above and left: two extreme examples of Bettie's home-made costumes.

fetishist, but she enjoyed doing it because she was "young and open to new experiences." Bettie says the craziest thing she ever did was to wear a full-length leather pony costume complete with head. "It was all a part of the posing, and posing was a very natural thing to me," she says of the bondage modeling. "I got a kick out of it. But I never thought those pictures would

have such a lasting effect."

Paula believes that Bettie remains an icon because she was a natural. "Her face. Her look. Her eyes. When she wanted to be dominant, she knew how to be dominant. And when she wanted to be seductive or passive, she could make you believe it. She could've been an actress. She had all the right looks. You didn't have to tell her. Sometimes Irving would direct — put your hand here, do this or look like this — but she knew just what to do."

Bettie perfected her high-spirited style of posing working for the Klaws. "I was always worried about doing a good job. I never played favorites with any of the photographers. Each time, I did my best."

No matter how complex the shot, or how dangerous it looked, Bettie remembers the bondage sessions as relaxed and safe. "I would never be afraid of Paula," she says. Only once in all the hundreds of sessions was Bettie uncomfortable. She played the victim bound in a highly intricate trussing, lifted from a hoist that left her dangling helplessly off the ground. "Irving had me tied around the waist and the legs, and my legs were spread apart, and my arms were tied up to a pulley. It frightened me because I thought it was going to pull the sockets out of my arms. My feet were off the ground, and I was tied to some posts with ropes from my feet and from the waist. It was just the idea of it." But according to Bettie, she was never tied up for long. Paula and Irving staged the scenes and took the photos right away. When reviewing the old photographs, Bettie laughs at her own seriousness in some of them. "Gee, I look like I'm in agony." But she doesn't laugh about the one in which she

Left and above: A rare, outdoor bondage sequence.

Right: A giddy Bettie gleefully escapes the clutches of her captors.

BETTIE PAGE

We now present a new Chained Girl 16mm silent movie called "Betty Page In Chains." This movie shows Betty Page attired in Leopard Skin Bikini outfit, and bare feet. Betty is very insubordinate and her mistress, portrayed by Roz Greenwood, then chains Betty to a chair, and Betty promises to be good and obey. Roz commands her to obey and comb her hair, when Betty pulls Roz's hair. Then Roz spanks Betty. This movie runs 100 feet in length and is well lighted with several close-ups. The price is only $14.00 for the complete movie. Roz is attired in Black Chemise, Black Stockings and wearing 6 inch High Heel Shoes.

Bettie plays victim to the "cruel" Roz Greenwood, another favorite Klaw model, in the short loop, *Betty Page in Chains*.

Dark Angel • 155

Shot during the filming of the short film *Captured Jungle Girl*, this session produced the all-time biggest selling photographs in the Klaw catalogues. Bettie declares that this was the single bondage shoot in which she was actually afraid. "I wasn't faking it in those pictures." Estes Kefauver exhibited complex bondage shots like these as evidence against Irving Klaw in his 1955 investigation into purveyors of "lewd" materials. Kefauver attempted to link a bondage photograph of Bettie to the mysterious alleged auto-erotic asphyxiation death of a 17 year-old Florida Eagle Scout.

Movie #90 "CAPTURED JUNGLE GIRL"

Our new bondage movie called "Captured Jungle Girl" features popular model Betty Page attired in leopard bra and Bikini style panties, being captured by new model Sima Cairo. The movie opens with Betty being captured and Sima then prepares an elaborate network of ropes and pulley gadgets to which Betty is bound securely and gagged and then raised completely off the floor while spreadeagled hands and feet. This movie comes in 2 parts of 100 feet each part and sells for $15.00 each part or $28.00 for the complete movie plus postage. Sima Cairo is attired in bra and pantie outfit and wears dark stockings. There are several close ups in this new type of bondage movie.

W-827   W-828   W-833   W-840   W-842   W-859
Scenes from Movie #90 "Captured Jungle Girl" featuring Betty Page as "Jungle Girl".
Photos illustrated above are 40¢ each photo.

was afraid. "I wasn't faking an expression on that one."

Bettie never thought the fetish and bondage modeling was lurid or wrong. It was all part of a job she enjoyed and did well. She was a freethinker in an era of conformity. Unlike other bohemian women, she didn't attach herself to well-known male artists or writers to seek fame or to become their personal muse. She didn't consider herself a pioneer, a feminist or a trendsetter. She had no agenda; she simply followed her own liberated instincts. "I wasn't trying to be anything," she insists. "I was just myself."

In the New York days, despite all the people she met and worked with, Bettie

Below: "Where did I get those cones? That looks like something Madonna would wear!" Opposite: Jack Kramer (Paula Klaw's husband), Bettie, Irving, Paula and model June King pose with their host after the group shot a bondage session at his house in upstate New York.

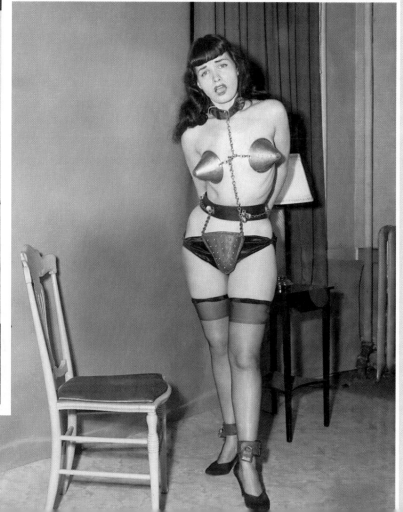

158

A potpourri of spanking shots. Bettie was equally adept at playing the spanker or the spanked.

remained true to her self-described lone-wolf personality. She did pal around for a time with another Klaw model, the red-haired beauty June King. But they didn't spend too much time together because June was married. Bettie simply didn't have many friends in New York. She didn't feel ostracized by other women who were more in line with the conservative sexual mores of the day. She simply didn't have much occasion to meet women like that. Rather than cultivate girl-

BETTIE PAGE

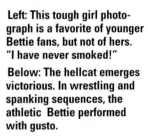

Left: This tough girl photograph is a favorite of younger Bettie fans, but not of hers. "I have never smoked!"

Below: The hellcat emerges victorious. In wrestling and spanking sequences, the athletic Bettie performed with gusto.

Nyack, New York. Summer 1953. Bettie in front of the ice-cream shop where she and fellow thespians took breaks from their work at the Sea Cliff Summer Theatre.

friends, Bettie worked out at the athletic club, sewed costumes for her jobs and indulged in her favorite activities: going to movies and reading fiction. "I was very interested in horror stories when I was in New York. I bought a great big book called *Tales of Terror and the Supernatural*, and I pored over that thing for hours and was scared to death by some of the terrible things I read. I was also into horror movies in those days." She also loved detective stories and read Sherlock Holmes, Raymond Chandler and Erle Stanley Gardner.

In 1953 Bettie enrolled in acting classes at Herbert Berghof's studio on the corner of 23rd Street and Sixth Avenue, which he ran with his wife, well-known Broadway actress Uta Hagen. Every Monday evening Bettie attended a workshop with approximately 50 other aspiring actors anxious to learn the Stanislavsky method from Berghof, its highly respected practitioner. Berghof assigned to the students a scene, which they rehearsed during the week and presented in the next class. Bettie's apartment often served as the

IT'S FOR HIM—Lovely Bettie Page, a young dramatic actress, was on hand in New York to present the coveted James Nixon Award to artist Charles Douglas. With an appraising eye, Douglas seems fully aware that Bettie would make a very good subject for a portrait.

BETTIE PAGE

Summer Theatre

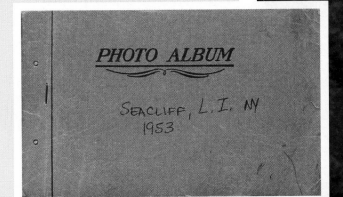

PHOTO ALBUM

SEACLIFF, L.I. NY
1953

site of the rehearsals. Sometimes the group went out for coffee, or in Bettie's case, milk, at a neighborhood cafe.

She performed a memorable scene from the one-act play *The Dark Lady of the Sonnets* with Robert Culp, who later landed the starring role in the television series *I Spy*. Under Berghof, Bettie became a devotee of Stanislavsky. "You can get quite a number of realities from the method. In *The Dark Lady of the Sonnets*, I played a lady-in-waiting to Queen Elizabeth. She was going to have me beheaded for making love to her lover, and I didn't know how I was going to get the reality of that. So I tried to think of something from my life I could use.

"When the scene was over, Mr. Berghof jumped up. He was so excited. He said, 'Bettie, what did you do to get the reality?' And I told him that I thought of what Jesus might do to me for all my sins. He couldn't believe that I was able to create such reality over something like that." Berghof encouraged her to pursue a professional career and recommended pieces in the workshop appropriate for her, including scenes from

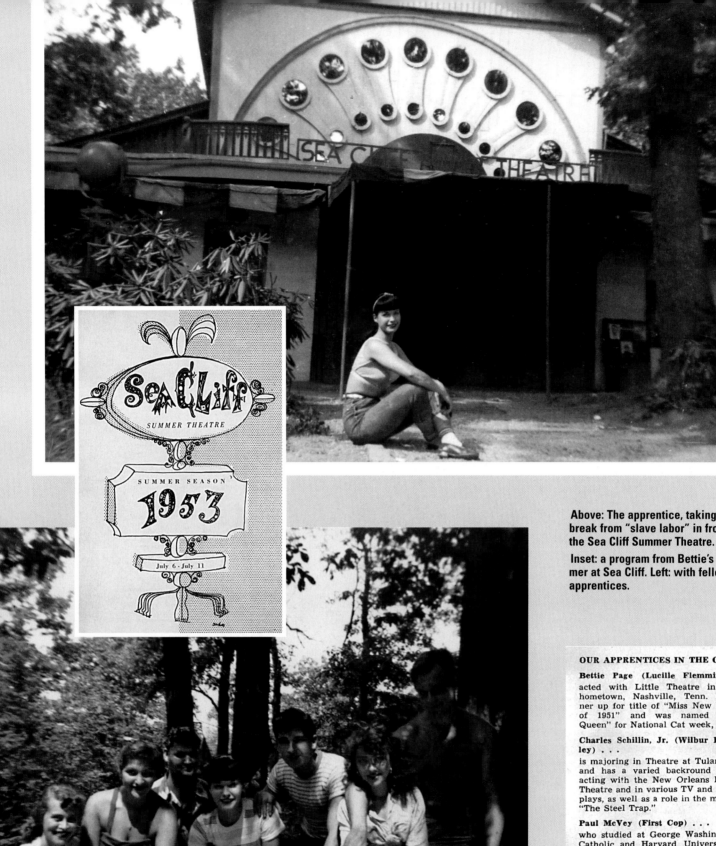

SUMMER SEASON
1953
July 6 - July 11

Above: The apprentice, taking a break from "slave labor" in front of the Sea Cliff Summer Theatre.

Inset: a program from Bettie's summer at Sea Cliff. **Left:** with fellow apprentices.

OUR APPRENTICES IN THE CAST

Bettie Page (Lucille Flemming)... acted with Little Theatre in her hometown, Nashville, Tenn. Runner up for title of "Miss New York of 1951" and was named "Cat Queen" for National Cat week, 1951.

Charles Schillin, Jr. (Wilbur Bentley) . . . is majoring in Theatre at Tulane U. and has a varied backround from acting with the New Orleans Little Theatre and in various TV and radio plays, as well as a role in the movie, "The Steel Trap."

Paul McVey (First Cop) . . . who studied at George Washington, Catholic and Harvard Universities, has appeared in college theatricals and at the Arena Theatre, Washington, D.C.

Tony Campo (Second Cop) . . . is a senior at Pace College where he is editor of the school paper and president of the Drama Society.

BETTIE PAGE

Top: The Glen Cove Inn was a popular dining spot before Sea Cliff's performances.

Above: Bettie with Tony Campo. "My fraternity brothers are still talking about the fact that I brought Bettie Page to one of our parties."

Right: Summer 1953: Campo and Bettie at his family's summer house in Goshen, New York, with his younger brother.

Trips
Home

Above: Bettie and her sister Goldie relaxing on the beach at Coney Island during one of Goldie's visits to New York. Right: On a trip home to Nashville, Bettie made this dress from fabric her sister Joyce had intended for curtains, until Joyce's puppy chewed the edges.

166

BETTIE PAGE

THEY ADMIRE HIM AT TENNESSEE, TOO—Huge Doug Atkins, 240 pounds of University of Tennessee tackle, is admired by a bevy of maidens at Cascade Plunge yesterday as the strapping Humboldt, Tenn., native from a bit of swimming relaxation. The pretty girls are (clockwise from lower left): Bettie Joe Waddell, Bettie Page, Joyce Wallace, Jan Hilton and Marian Marks.

—Staff Photo by Jack Hows

Above left: at Cascade Plunge, a public swimming pool at the Nashville Fairgrounds, Bettie feels the muscles of Chicago Bears tackle Doug Atkins, formerly a University of Tennessee football hero. To Atkins' right is Bettie's sister Joyce. Above: Bettie with her sister-in-law Gladys Page. Left: Bettie and Joyce. "I always thought Joyce was prettier than me. She had beautiful, natural blonde hair. She should have been the model."

Tennessee Williams. He never tried to change her, or make her lose her Southern accent. Berghof pleaded with her to audition for the Broadway production of *Li'l Abner,* thinking she would be perfect for Moonbeam McSwine, the role that pin-up favorite Julie Newmar landed in the movie. "But I didn't think I had a chance, so I didn't go. I was sort of backward about auditioning for things. I never tried out for the plays that I saw advertised. If I had, I think I could have done something on Broadway."

Lack of ambition didn't stop Bettie from auditioning for an apprenticeship at Sea Cliff Summer Theatre on Long Island in 1953. It was an illustrious season; the theater mounted the original production of *Cabin in the Sky* with music performed by Billy Strayhorn, Duke Ellington's partner and arranger, and Luther Henderson. And Ethel Waters performed

Bettie poses with her mother, Edna Page, during her trips back home. Bettie and Edna remained close during Bettie's modeling years, and Bettie would often send home money. "I wanted to help Momma after all she'd done to keep us together as a family when we were children."

BETTIE PAGE

Clockwise: Bettie with Edna at the Cascade Plunge pool; with Gladys and Edna at Rock City in Chattanooga, Tennessee; with Joyce and Gladys.

her one-woman show, *At Home With Ethel Waters*. Although apprentices didn't get major roles, Bettie did play one of the bathing beauties in *Gentlemen Prefer Blondes* and a young prostitute in Tennessee Williams' *Camino Reál*. She served as prop mistress on a production of *Bell, Book and Candle*, starring Alexis Smith and Victor Jory.

That season Bettie met Tony Campo, a fellow actor and Pace College senior with a list of extracurricular activities to match her own. Campo was a student council officer, editor of the school newspaper and president of both the dramatics club and his fraternity. He lived in the Bronx with his large Italian family; Bettie, who had always wanted such a

clan, was smitten with them. "He had oodles of relatives who'd come to dinner. His mother would cook great big platters of spaghetti and all kinds of fascinating Italian dishes. I liked his family very much. They were very loving."

"I'll never forget the time I took Bettie to a family dinner on Staten Island," Campo recalls. "We were going swimming — now it was the Fifties, remember — and Bettie came out of the bathroom wearing the tiniest bikini. Of course she looked great in it, but everyone's jaw dropped. They still talk about it."

Campo's family liked Bettie. Though she was a pin-up model and sex symbol, he says Bettie was the kind of girl one took home to

$1.00 Bizarre N° 14

Left: *Bizarre* Magazine, 1954. This publication was the brainchild of fetish artist John Coutts, known as John Willie, creator of the famous bondage comic serial *Sweet Gwendoline*. *Bizarre* featured Willie's photographs and illustrations of women in often graphic bondage scenarios.

Below: Fetish in Technicolor.

meet the folks: entirely genuine, intelligent and utterly unique. "If you think Bettie was an exhibitionist in her personal life — no way! She usually dressed in rolled-up jeans, penny loafers, socks and sweaters. In fact, she liked my brother's lumberjack shirt so much I stole it and gave it to her." Still, according to Campo, Bettie was unorthodox. "Bettie used to do her laundry in the bathtub — while she bathed!" he recalls with amused affection. "Her attitude was, 'Why waste the water?'" They dated for a year until Campo went into the service in June 1954. "I was her 'other life,'" he says. He knew all about her profession, but true to the furtive spirit of the 1950s they barely discussed it. "I used to see her pictures in magazines," he says, "so I knew everything, but it didn't matter to me."

Bettie visited Campo's family in upstate New York at their summer home in Goshen, and in New York City they went to the movies, walked in Central Park and dined on hamburgers. Campo says that Bettie was content to do what starving college students did for entertainment. An enthusiastic chef and baker, she cooked for them at her apartment — and Campo verifies that her cooking was excellent. He had no money, but Bettie

Though Bettie never worked as a strip-teaser or danced in burlesque shows, she appeared in three burlesque films — *Striporama, Teaserama* and *Varietease.* Inspired by the success of the first, produced by Martin Lewis, Irving Klaw produced the two others. Tame by today's standards, the films were considered racy in the 1950s. Right: *Striporama* starred Lili St. Cyr, "The World's Most Beautiful Woman," and featured Mrs. America, burlesque comics Mandy Kaye and Jack Diamond, plus Rosita "and her trained pigeons." Below: Bettie steps out of the bathtub in *Striporama.*

FOR THE FIRST TIME IN COLOR
The most exotic stars in ONE GREAT SHOW!

NOMINATED BEST ADULT SHOW OF THE YEAR!
—International Pin-Up Girls Association

3 BIG HITS!

All In

LILI ST. CYR
GEORGIA SOTHERN
ROSITA ROYCE

STRIPORAMA

IN COLOR FOR THE 1ST TIME!
with BETTY PAGE · JACK DIAMOND
Mr. & Mrs. AMERICA
and THE VENUS BEAUTIES

AND SEE — "CINDERELLA'S LOVE LESSON"

PLUS!

didn't care. One night when he waited for her in her apartment, he looked out the window and saw her emerge from a huge black limousine. She explained that she'd been out with a rich Texan who liked to take her to dinner when he was in town. Campo says it was obvious that Bettie could have had a wealthy boyfriend or husband, but she just didn't care about money. "She was content to eat hot dogs at the park. She wasn't a restaurant girl. She didn't even drink. We were just like a couple of kids together.

"Bettie loved to hop in the car and just drive. So one night I got my father's car and we took off. We drove so far out that Bettie finally said, 'Let's just stop and go to sleep.' And we did. She slept in the front seat and I slept in the back, and when we woke up in the morning in the middle of nowhere, we just turned around and drove back. But that was Bettie. Those little spontaneous things pleased her." Campo says that she looked stylish in anything she wore. He remembers her riding the subway in high heels and a wide black

BETTIE

Right: Bettie's scene in *Striporama* was billed as "the most daring bath scene ever filmed," though she wore a white bikini in the tub. The press release for the film boasted of her fame as a nationally known pin-up in a "startling performance" and allowed that despite her success as a leading pin-up, Bettie, an accomplished singer and dancer, yearned for roles in legitimate theater.

belt — a look that he says would be very chic and provocative today. "Everyone looked," he says.

Naomi Caryl, formerly Naomi Hirshhorn, a fellow apprentice at Sea Cliff, recalls that everyone at the theater thought Bettie was gorgeous, and that all the men were tongue-tied in her presence. According to Caryl, Bettie miraculously won permission from the producers to take two days off during the week to go into New York City. The other apprentices were jealous that Bettie managed to avoid two days of slave labor. One of them spread the rumor that she had a secret life posing for "naughty pictures." Caryl says she was a terribly naive 20-year-old at the time, "as naive as one could be and still be in the theater," and didn't believe that someone as beautiful, sweet and virginal looking as Bettie could possibly do such a thing for a living. "Bettie was a classy woman. She brought a wholesomeness to her work. That's probably what made her the icon she is."

Top: Irving Klaw buys the first ticket for his movie, *Varietease*. Released in 1954, *Varietease* featured Bettie in an Arabian costume (right); which she peels off to reveal an abbreviated version of the same. The film was a big success for Klaw.

Opposite top: Bettie, Irving and an unidentified man at a New York restaurant the night *Varietease* opened.

According to Caryl, Bettie looked 20 years old though she was 30 and had already been married and divorced. "Bettie had a lot of parts that summer," Campo adds, "but — funny — she always played the beautiful young girl." Even Campo didn't know how old Bettie was until recently. "There was no doubt in my mind that we were the same age," he says, though his mother — using maternal radar — cautioned him that Bettie was probably older than he thought.

Back from Sea Cliff, Bettie continued her studies with Berghof. With his encouragement, she landed several roles in the New York theater and made four appearances on television. She was in various off-Broadway

Bettie signs photos in the theater lobby at the *Varietease* premiere.

Left: At the *Varietease* premiere.
Below: Irving Klaw on opening night.

Below: Bettie promotes *Varietease* on WABC radio in New York. Paul Hartman, the well-known performer sits at Bettie's left. The other two men are unidentified.

productions including *3* at The Playhouse on 78th Street in January of 1956; and *Time Is a Thief*, with Richard Kennan and Darnay Pierre at Manhattan's Finch Playhouse. In *Sunday Costs Five Pesos*, a comedy by Josephine Niggli at a theater in the Village, she played Berta, an 18-year-old girl. "I don't know how convincing I was in that part, but it got pretty good notices. We got good audiences, and Mr. Berghof came to see it and liked it a lot."

In 1955 Bettie appeared as "Miss Pin-Up Girl of the World" on the Earl Wilson television show. She landed a small dramatic part on the weekly series *Eye Witness* and another on an episode of *The U.S. Steel Hour* in a play

dramatic part of any length that I had on TV. I don't remember how I got those two parts, since I never made the rounds to the T.V. studios. I think Mr. Berghof helped." Bettie also appeared on *The Jackie Gleason Show*, but she doesn't have fond memories of the Great One. "He was a tyrant, screaming and yelling all the time. He treated everyone on the set like slaves. He was a real cad."

Hillard "Hilly" Elkins, the well-known former MCA agent who also produced *Oh Calcutta!* on Broadway, managed several starlets in New York in the 1950s. Bettie came to his attention when he saw her in one of the off-Broadway shows. Elkins and Berghof were friends, and Berghof urged him to sign her to a contract. "He was thinking of managing me, but I told him my real age," Bettie says. "And Mr. Berghof said, 'Bettie, you talk too much.'"

Bettie continued with acting classes but by her own admission, she failed to dedicate herself to acting professionally. Despite Berghof's encouragement and the theater and television appearances, she didn't try to get an agent, call on producers or attend auditions. "I was just satisfied for myself that I could act after I had studied it for three years. I felt like I could act, and yet I didn't make any effort to be an actress."

about illegal aliens crossing into Texas from Mexico. She played the role of Carmelita, a Mexican girl crossing the Rio Grande with several others and landing in jail. In retrospect, she marvels that the director encouraged her to play the role without changing her Southern accent. "It was the only good

Right: The young French maid attends to her mistress, Tempest Storm, in a scene from *Teaserama*. These renowned photos led fans to believe that Bettie and Tempest worked together often and were friends, but they met only once, during the filming of the movie. "I really liked Tempest. She was so sweet and easy to work with. I remember Paula Klaw holding Tempest's little pooch while we shot that day." Later in the film, Bettie mocks Tempest as she preens, and when Tempest catches her at it, she pulls Bettie's hair.

Zipping undies add zip to the movie.

These Misses are hits in filmusical "Teaserama." Left, Betty Paige (in part of maid) straightens curls of star Tempest Storm.

TEASERAMA

Sauciest cinema of the century, "Teaserama " is 4-stare film fare revealing country's top exotics. It makes bow in N. Y. in Feb., should win the Anatomy Award for '55.

A still from Bettie's dance solo in *Teaserama*. She designed and sewed her own costume for the movie.

MEET THE GIRLS
VOL. 1   NO. 3

Special —
Bettie Page
and Friends

JUDY O'DAY   BETTIE PAGE

All new photos of your pin-up favorites—for photographers and art students

BLACK STOCKING
.... PARADE

featuring ....   No. 2

Bettie Page

Bettie's fetish cult began to build while she still worked. In addition to posing for the Klaws she appeared in the digest-size, slick, fetish magazines that specialized in presenting the domina-trix, and appealed to more serious S & M aficionados.

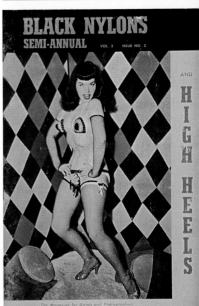

BETTIE PAGE

Left: From the specialty fetish magazine *Focus on Bettie Page*.

FLORIDA APR. 1954

Trips to Florida

During the seven years from 1950 to 1957 that Bettie Page modeled in New York, she took several extended trips to Florida. At least once a year, she fled the cold weather and traveled to visit her youngest sister in Miami. Bettie loved the beach and the sun. She went to Florida to rest, not work. But when word spread that New York's top pin-up was in town, photographers came calling.

Bettie posed for H. W. Hannau, Jan Caldwell, Bunny Yeager, Benno Correa and others. Several of Hannau's photos of Bettie became a series of popular postcards. He convinced her to climb craggy rocks barefooted for the shoot; she still winces when she views those photographs.

When Bettie wasn't modeling, she spent time in Matheson Hammock Park, a favorite hangout of the University of Miami crowd. "I would go swimming across a channel that was dug very deep for boats to go through. There were boats going back and forth all the time, and yet I would swim across. I could easily have been hit. But I was a good swimmer, and I was determined to get across the channel to this nice little beach, which was full of mango trees."

In 1954 the Miami columnist Herb Rau introduced Bettie to Bunny Yeager, a local model turned photographer. Yeager had just started selling her pictures to pin-up magazines and Bettie, a well-known New York City model, agreed to shoot with her, often free of charge when Yeager couldn't afford to pay her. "Sometimes she paid me as little as five dollars. Once she

Opposite page: This scorchingly sexy shot became a postcard with an open-jawed alligator superimposed behind the unsuspecting Bettie. The copy read, "Wow! We alligators do have fun in New Orleans." On Florida postcards, the alligators had "fun in the Florida Keys."

Above: Bettie in a snapshot off Florida's coast. She wrote on the back to her mother, "On the spot where this was taken, you and I basked in the sun — and cold wind — that day in December."

one of the major reasons I loved working with her. I was expressing myself with her body instead of mine.

"Bettie was like a comic strip come to life: unreal, but real. She seemed so perfect: flawless tanned skin and a beautiful, well-structured face. One of the things I noticed about her the first time she stepped into my studio was that when she took off her clothes, she never seemed naked. Her tan was all over — it seemed almost like it was airbrushed on her. Her skin was perfect — no blemishes. Perfect nose; beautiful straight teeth, and gleaming, shiny black hair that was always in place, always."

Yeager photographed Bettie at Africa USA, a jungle-style petting zoo. Nude and also wearing a leopard costume, Bettie posed with a menagerie of animals — cheetahs, snakes, zebras and more. The night before, she had a scare and the famous shoot almost didn't happen. She lived on Sixth Street near the river in downtown Miami in the guest cottage of a secluded and private estate. The landlord was away for the weekend, and Bettie was sewing in the main house finishing the leopard skin outfit for the next day's shoot. Past midnight Bettie locked up the

even gave me a little three-dollar makeup kit as compensation. But I liked her." The combination of Bettie's beauty and Yeager's camera produced some of Bettie's most memorable pictures.

In the Yeager photographs Bettie is almost always outdoors: on a boat, in the ocean, in a jungle setting or on the beach. She looks fresh and alive — the all-American girl frolicking in the sun. "They said I looked happy in the water and I was. I was happy cavorting around stark naked on the beach," says Bettie.

Yeager explains Bettie's appeal: "Bettie Page was number one. I have never known another model who had a better knowledge of her body or how to work with it to make it look so good. When I met Bettie I recognized the same qualities and creativity in her that I had myself. She knew instinctively what I wanted without me having to demonstrate it like I had to do with other models. It was like dancing with someone. Sometimes you find a partner who moves exactly like you do. There is no leader — it's hard to describe. This is

Left: A moody nude shot by Florida photographer Jan Caldwell.
Below: Even during the winter months, Bettie couldn't stay away from the beach.

BETTIE PAGE

house and walked along the path to her cottage. "I got to the cottage and was undressing, when all of a sudden I heard scratching sounds," Bettie recollects. "I froze when I realized it was somebody at my window. I cut the light, and when I went up to the window, there was a huge black form taking the screen off. I don't know where I got pres-

Above: One of the many postcard shots by Florida photographer H. W. Hannau.

ence of mind, but all of a sudden I said, 'I'll give you two seconds to get away from this window or I'll blow your brains out!'" The man dropped the screen and ran away. Bettie screamed, running to the night watchman who took care of the boats docked by the river. She stayed with him for hours, then stayed awake in the main house until dawn, afraid to return to the cottage.

Yeager showed up at seven-thirty in the morning as planned. Bettie hadn't slept a wink and was still shaken. "I looked terrible, as if I had been on a big drunk or something. I didn't want to take the pictures. But Bunny kept insisting that she arranged for the location that morning, and she made me go. I thought I looked terrible in the pictures. I had big bags under my eyes in all of them. But she sold nearly every one of them, and she didn't even retouch them."

From the specialty magazine *Bettie Page Outdoors*, a publication devoted to Bettie on the beach and in the water. Photographs by Bunny Yeager.

Four postcards by H. W. Hannau. The upper left photo was issued as a novelty postcard and as a squeak toy. When Bettie's belly was squeezed, it let out a whistle.

BETTIE PAGE

★ ASK A DOZEN picture editors who the World's Champion Pinup Girl is, and at least ten of them will answer: Bettie Page, also known as Betty Paige, Bette Page, and Bettie Paige. But no matter how you write it, this girl spells "oomph" in big round capitals!

Bettie's smile is brighter than Florida sunshine.

14

While Yeager continues to capitalize on Bettie's image with books, trading cards and other merchandise, she won't allow Bettie to see the photos or own copies of them unless Bettie, who lives on Social Security, agrees to pay $200 for each 8 x 10 print. "What has Bettie Page done for me lately?" she said in response to a personal letter from Bettie asking to use photos in this book. "Bettie pays like everybody else."

"I just don't understand," says Bettie, shaking her head. "I was happy to help her." Bunny's lack of generosity seems an ungracious denial of her debt to Bettie Page. According to pin-up scholar Bob Schultz, "Without Bettie, there'd be little interest in Bunny today. Without Bunny, Bettie would still be a star."

In April 1954 Bettie walked along White Street in Key West and spotted a young man in a white pullover shirt, looking out to sea. Even from behind, before she saw his face, she was attracted to him. "He must have sensed I was there looking at him because he turned around. I asked him to take a picture of me. He was so nervous that the pictures were very blurred. I went for a swim and two of his buddies came along. They started talking to me, but I was interested in him, not them. He was so shy that he didn't say anything. Finally one of his brothers came along in a car, and he got in. I thought I would never see him again, so I said, 'Where are you going?' And he said, 'Home.' 'Would you like to go out with me?' I asked. His eyes lit up, and he stammered, 'Yes!' He said, 'I thought you were interested in my friends.' I said, 'No, I'm interested in you.'" They went to a drive-in movie that weekend

For five solid years Bettie has been the country's most popular pinup.

A Swedish sculptor offered her $10,000 if she'd go to Sweden to pose.

Bettie is offered more modeling jobs

than she can handle. It is estimated that she earns $15,000 a year!

And she wants to act? . . .

Reason for the variations in spelling may be that photographers, befuddled by Bettie's special radiance, forgot to ask about orthography when it came to getting down the vital statistics. They didn't forget to note, though, that Bette has long blue-black hair, a petite 5′ 3″ body which measures, in the important

16

17

In her spare time she studies dance.   She's an expert swimmer and diver.

There are hundreds of good models, but only one Bettie Page!

places, 36-23-35, electric-blue eyes, and a smile that could warm a penguins tail-feathers. Unfortunately, nature's gift to the world of pinups, may not be available much longer. Bettie has contracted a serious interest in acting, and has moved her center of operations from the photogenically sunlit strands of Florida to

the neon-lit canyons of New York. She's already made her first New York stage appearance, starring in an off-Broadway production called *Dramarena*. Now she has hopes that she may be signed to do a Broadway play. But the dramatic arts can't cover up the fact that her pinup artistry is still the best "Page" in her life.

18

19

Opposite page and right: Recently discovered photos by 1950s pin-up hobbyist and jet-setter, the late Benno Correa. Correa was the only child of a wealthy merchant family from the Netherlands Antilles who got involved in photography in the 1930s. With his wife Gladys he traveled the world, living in Havana during the city's heyday, and at the center of New York cafe society. "He was a Latin in Manhattan," says his son, Dexter. "Quite the glamorous figure." Benno had a studio at his family's estate in Connecticut where models came to shoot with him on the idyllic grounds. Correa shot Bettie in both New York and Miami. With the resurgence of interest in pin-up art, his photography is receiving the attention it deserves.

Below: Correa photographing a model in his studio.

MODEL CHAMP? — Betty has appeared on so many covers and in so many magazines as a pinup, that she is generally considered to be the country's top pinup model today. This Bunny Yeager photo shows the freshness and charm which put Betty on top.

Above and below: Postcard shots by Hannau. Bettie winces when she looks at these pictures. "I'll never forget climbing on those sharp rocks. My feet hurt just thinking about those shots."

and stayed out until five o'clock in the morning.

"He didn't even know how to kiss," Bettie recalls with affection. "The first time I kissed him, he just pushed his lips up against mine. That's all he knew. He had never even had sex with a woman. I taught him everything. But once he learned what it was all about, you couldn't stop him!" He was 18; Bettie was 31. Four years later the boy on the beach, Armond Walterson, became Bettie's second husband.

Despite her romance with Armond and her popularity with Florida photographers, Bettie always returned to New York City, where she continued to date admirers. She was more interested in regular

FLORIDA APR. 1954

FLORIDA APR. 1954

Opposite page: On her toes, shot by Florida photographer Bill Hamilton.

Below: Bettie's caption for this 1954 snapshot read, "If they ever have a contest to determine the world's greatest smoocher, this guy will be way up in the running." Left: Bettie wrote on the back to Edna, "These were taken at Matheson-Hammock Beach, where I took you once; remember?"

guys — college men, aspiring actors and enlisted men. She never dated the photographers, and she thwarted the advances of the rich and famous who tried to entice her with gifts and glamour. Incredibly, Bettie insists that she had trouble meeting men during her modeling days. She claims that men never approached her on the street or in public places. She appeared in scores of men's magazines, but she believed she was virtually unrecognizable in person. "When I wasn't going to a job, I didn't wear any make-up and I wore jeans and an old floppy sweater. Nobody recognized me.

"I think most men were afraid of models who had any kind of name or reputation. Several actors I dated expressed the opinion that men thought I was above them. They didn't try to go out with me because I was a well-known model and they were unknown." But they were wrong. The night *Teaserama* opened, Bettie invited Tony Campo, on leave from the Army, to be her date. They watched the movie together from the back row, and then Bettie greeted her fans and signed autographs in the lobby. Campo says that though Bettie was the celebrity and he was "just a skinny pri-

FLORIDA APR. 1954

vate, a nobody," she never sent the signal that he, or anyone else, was beneath her. "She didn't act like she shouldn't be seen with me because I was just a lowly private. Afterwards I took her home and said good night. It was the last time I ever saw her."

For three years Bettie had an on-again, off-again relationship with fellow Berghof student Marvin Greene. A handsome blond, says Bettie, Marvin always positioned himself to look taller than her — even when they sunbathed side by side on the beach. Bettie introduced him to camping, which he loved. They bought equipment and traveled together for two summers through New England, Canada and Nova Scotia.

Bettie dated others in New York, though not seriously. Richard Arbib, an artist, futurist and auto designer, was one of her boyfriends. He joked with her that he designed the Hamilton Triangle Ventura I watch for her because of her

Florida's most exportable item, beauty, is exemplified by exquisite model Betty Page.

Though Bettie visited Florida to rest and enjoy the sun, she worked relentlessly while there. All photos this page by Jan Caldwell.

Overleaf: The best single image of Bettie ever shot by Caldwell.

Photographed for
MAN'S MAGAZINE
by JAN CALDWELL

PAGE FOR THE MEMORY BOOK

*Famous Bettie Page, as refreshing
as the breezes of Summertime
and the winds of Spring.
A rose pressed in an old book,
a lover's kiss, a sigh. . . . .*

FLORIDA APR. 1954

Upper right: "His name is John — a real nice boy, captain of the swimming team at the University of Miami. He liked me a lot, but I just couldn't see dating him because he wasn't even as tall as I am in my bare feet!" Above left, right and opposite page: Photographs by Bunny Yeager.

Blithe Savage

Don't think for a minute that the jungle abounds with cuties like this. That pretty hair-do and that naughty little leopard skin are products of a complex civilization. Of course, what lies underneath is both civilized and primitive, depending on her mood. And the mood here is a pretty blend of female fact and fancy.

Our smiling savage displays primitive woman's fondness for light clothing as well as an affection for furry animals. Her sophisticated sisters have the same urges and satisfy them with bikinis and mink. For proof that our jungle girl is both a lady and a sprite — see right. When dressing for town, she never forgets her parasol and long formal gloves.

perennial tardiness. They stayed in touch by letter until Arbib passed away in early 1995.

According to Bettie, she refused to date men to advance her career. She met with a producer from Columbia Pictures who was shooting a western in South Dakota. He said he wanted her to star in the movie, but, "He told me pointblank, 'You have to be nice to me in order to get the part.' Now, he was a crummy-looking thing," she laughs, "and I didn't want him touching me at all, so I told him no. He got very angry. He jumped up off the couch and said, 'You'll be sorry. I can get any number of girls who would be willing to be nice to me in order to have a lead in a movie.' I guess he could. But I didn't want to have anything to do with him."

Bettie's lack of golddigger instinct passed the ultimate test when she was summoned by the reclusive millionaire filmmaker Howard Hughes. Sometime in 1955 or 1956 Hughes' right-hand man telephoned Irving Klaw asking for Bettie's phone number. The man called her and asked her if she would like to go out with Hughes. "With all the things I

BETTIE PAGE

To be, or not to BI-KINI?

Above and right: From a special feature on Bettie in *Adam* magazine, 1956.

Glamor on the go—there's no rest for Betty as avid local lensmen close in . . .

67

Miss Irresistible

Gotham's busiest model headed for a Miami vacation rest—but Florida photogs had other ideas

MORE▶

had heard about him and all his women, I didn't want to date Howard Hughes. I just didn't care to meet him," Bettie says emphatically. "But then this fellow said, 'Well, Mr. Hughes wants to take a screen test of you, some photographs and some motion pictures.' So I went to a studio downtown, and they took several shots — profiles, front views, side views. But nothing ever came of it. I guess he wasn't interested after I wouldn't go out with him."

The End of an Era
Preparing to Walk Away

In 1955 Estes Kefauver, U.S. Senator and presidential aspirant from Bettie's home state of Tennessee, seized media attention by forming a Senate subcommittee to investigate the supposed link between pornography and juvenile delinquency. The committee targeted Irving Klaw, calling him "one of the largest distributors of obscene, lewd, and fetish photographs throughout the country by mail." Kefauver intended to prove that because 65 percent of the Klaws' mailing list consisted of juvenile girls who purchased still photographs of their favorite movie stars, the Klaws were also putting their "lewd" pin-up and fetish photographs into the hands of little girls. Politicians, concerned citizens and "experts" pleaded before the Kefauver committee to intervene on behalf of "the children," who had to be protected from "the floods of certain kinds of comic books and other pornographic material" which arouses in them "base emotion." These base emotions, the experts alleged, led directly to the menace of "juvenile delinquency." Kefauver called to testify a psychiatrist, Dr. George W. Henry from Cornell University Medical College, who declared the sole purpose of the Klaws' publication *Cartoon and Model Parade* was to "stimulate people erotically in an abnormal way." He assured the committee that exposure to such material could pervert children and teenagers.

The committee blamed the strange death, possibly auto-erotic asphyxiation, of

Above: The calm before the storm. Irving Klaw prepares for battle with Senator Estes Kefauver in the final days of his reign as Pin-Up King.

a 17-year-old Eagle Scout in Florida, Kenneth Grimm, on a bondage photograph of Bettie Page. His father found his body, tied up coincidentally in much the same position as one of Bettie's pictures. Based on the testimony of Mr. Grimm, Kefauver linked the picture, which the boy never saw, to his death. The committee summoned Irving.

"That was a shame," Bettie says, recalling how the government hounded the Klaws. "They thought Irving was doing pornography. I don't know where they got that idea! Irving didn't even do nudes. You couldn't even see any pubic hair or nipples through any of Irving's lingerie, bras and panties, or any other of his costumes." Bettie confirms the rumor that Irving was so careful that he had the models wear two pairs of underwear if he thought they were transparent.

One day two representatives from the Kefauver committee showed up at Bettie's front door. They told her it was time to admit that Irving was selling pornography, and that they intended to call her to testify

Above: Irving surrounded by four of his models. No matter how severe the shot, the Klaws maintained an atmosphere of levity. Below: "That was the strangest thing I ever had to do. I'll never forget it."

BETTIE PAGE

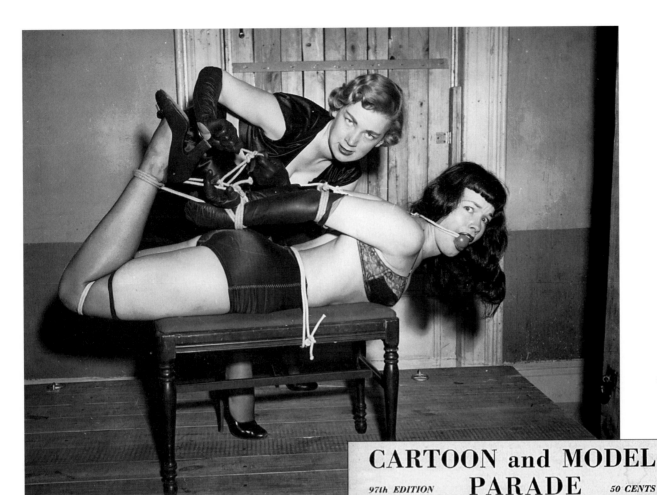

to that effect before the Senate committee. "I told them very frankly that Irving Klaw never did any pornography at all, not even nudes, and that I would say that if they put me on the stand." The men didn't offer Bettie a definition of pornography, which she assumed meant depictions of sex acts, sexual positions and open-legged poses. "I told them I didn't appreciate them saying these things about Irving. He was a very nice fellow, his models were never naked and there were never any men in the photographs. How could it be pornography?"

Nonetheless, the committee called Bettie to the United States Courthouse at Foley Square in New York City and forced her to sit in a small room, alone, for 16 hours. She wasn't allowed to leave. Finally, at her request, someone brought her a sandwich. Other than

This issue of *Cartoon and Model Parade* was used as evidence against Irving Klaw during the Kefauver hearings.

A typical scene from a Klaw bondage loop. The model's enthusiasm is apparent as she paddles Bettie's bottom for the camera.

rier business from 1932 to 1937. In his attempt to link Klaw with anything prurient, Kefauver demanded to know if the models who posed for Klaw's "lewd" pictures also posed for other photographers' pictures. He asked repeatedly if Klaw hired teenage girls to pose without producing either the name or the testimony of any such teenager. He produced no evidence that the juvenile girls who ordered movie star pictures from Klaw ever received anything other than those pictures. He subpoenaed Irving to bring in his "lewd" material, but again Irving refused to comply, taking the Fifth. Finally Kefauver dismissed him; the exposé failed. Transcripts of the hearings show that Kefauver called others before his committee and accused them of the same misdeeds. They, too, declined to answer his charges under immunity provisions of the Fifth Amendment of the Constitution.

As for Irving, his career as "Pin-Up King" declined along with his health after the investigations. Though dismissed by the Kefauver committee, for years to come the authorities hounded him through the postal code, which prohibited the mailing of "obscene" materials. Others, too, paid a price for their involvement with the Klaws. The man who owned the printing lab the Klaws used also worked for the Walt Disney Studios. According to Paula, Disney executives warned him during the Kefauver hearings that if he continued to work for the Klaws, he would no longer work for Disney.

The Klaws tried to play by the book. Irving wanted peace of mind, not only for himself and his sister, but for his business associates. In 1957, weary of the conflicts, he ceased production of pin-up and bondage photographs. Toward the end of the year, he called Bettie, and Paula remembers the conversation. "Irving said to her,

that, no one said a word to her.

The committee dismissed Klaw after he took the Fifth on every question. Frustrated, Kefauver questioned him relentlessly, threatening to hold him in contempt. On the advice of his lawyers, Coleman Gangel and Joseph E. Brill, Klaw refused to answer any questions other than where he lived, and that he was in the fur-

'Look Bettie, we have a little problem with the federal government. We're not going to shoot until we can straighten this out. I don't want you to think that I'm not calling you [for work] because we don't like you. You know we love you. I don't want you to get involved.' He was trying to protect her.

"That was it," Paula says with some bitterness. "We never worked again after that. Irving felt that it wasn't worth the harassment and the aggravation, and plus it cost an awful lot of money. Besides, it cost him his health. It made him very ill."

Irving encouraged Paula and her husband to open up a shop in New Jersey in another jurisdiction where he believed she wouldn't be harassed. In 1958 Paula and Jack Kramer opened the Nutrix Company in Jersey City. Irving stayed in the New York shop, selling only movie stills, memorabilia and celebrity photos while remaining a financial partner in Nutrix.

But in the early 1960s when Robert F. Kennedy was Attorney General, the government decided once again to crack down

Above: Manacled, leather-clad, blindfolded Bettie. "It was all part of the job." Inset: in 1960, Nutrix began repackaging some of Bettie's more outrageous bondage shoots as small digest photo booklets with accompanying text. Later volumes included wrestling and other fetish themes.

BETTY PAGE IN BONDAGE

VOLUME ONE

ILLUSTRATED WITH 25
Actual Photos of Betty Page

on "vice and smut," and federal agents raided the Nutrix Company, arresting Paula's husband and impounding boxes of inventory. On June 27, 1963, Irving Klaw and Jack Kramer were charged with conspiracy to send obscene materials through the mail. They were released that day on $10,000 bail. According to Paula, the warden at the jail told her off the record that he thought the idea of raiding her store was ridiculous, but he believed it was initiated by the Attorney General, so it had to be taken seriously. In light of recent revelations about the sex lives of the Kennedy brothers, Paula is amused at the irony of them as warriors against vice and smut.

In an effort to end his troubles forever, Irving struck a deal with the law: He agreed to shred almost all of his negatives. Irving insisted that Nutrix comply with the authorities to the letter of their demands, but Paula, in defiance and anger, preserved much of the original fetish material. She could only stand to shred so much of her own work, and she kept many of the original negatives of her friend and favorite model, Bettie Page.

Right: In an unusual outdoor shoot, a gleeful Bettie kidnaps, hogties and tosses her hapless victim (June King) in the trunk of a waiting sedan.

Below: Bettie finds herself on the receiving end in a similar scenario.

Disgusted, Irving decided to retire. "He really felt he wasn't doing anything wrong, and that he was being persecuted for nothing. So at that point he said, 'I'm going to Florida. Here — it's all yours, Paula. Do whatever you want.'" Irving gave the business to his sister and prepared to move. He planned to leave October

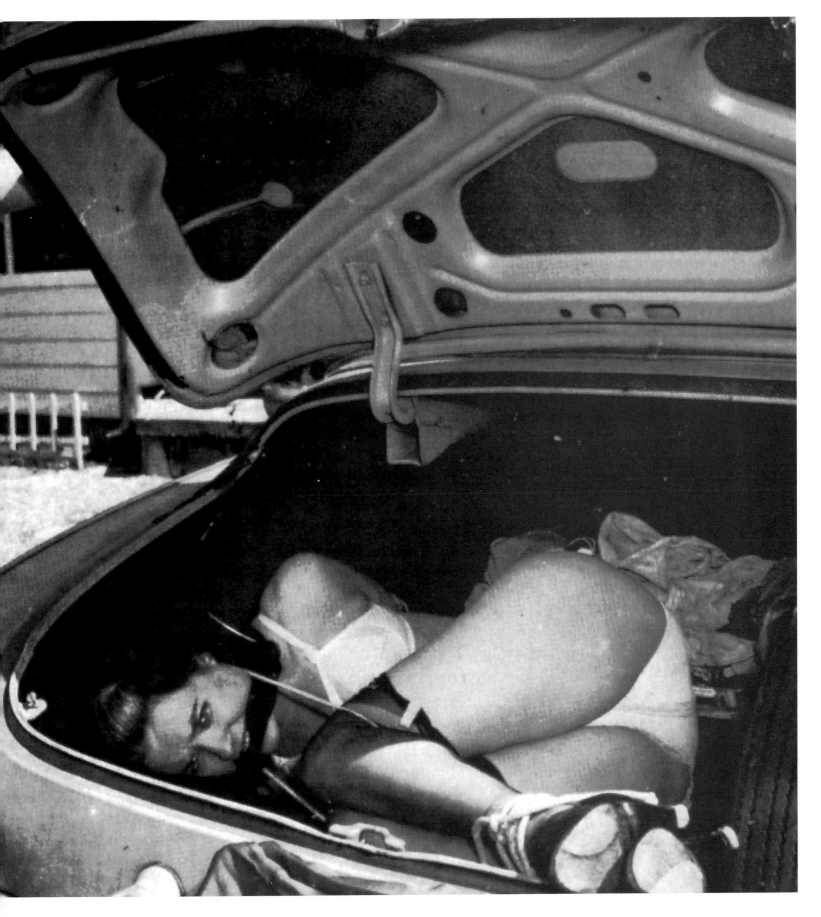

1st, but he never made it. One month before, he was diagnosed with a virus. During his examination, however, a ruptured appendix went undetected, and in 1966 he died of peritonitis. He was only 59 years old.

The government's treatment of the Klaws appalled Bettie, but she had bigger problems. In 1957 she received a series of typewritten, unsigned letters threatening her. The writer described his intentions in graphic detail. Among other things, he wanted to pull off her breasts with pliers. Worse, he let Bettie know that he had her under surveillance. He knew her whereabouts and what she wore on any given day.

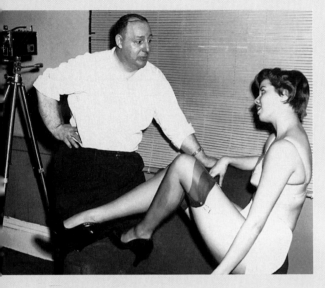

Pin-up auteur at work. Irving Klaw with one of his models.

Alarmed, Bettie took off to Nashville to stay with her mother. When she returned, a new stack of letters awaited her. She went to the police, who involved the FBI, who believed the perpetrator was a murderer who had thus far eluded them. "I was really frightened then," Bettie says. She agreed to cooperate with the police and the FBI in an attempt to trap the stalker. "In one of the last letters I received, this maniac ordered me to bring in an envelope a series of photographs of myself to the corner of One 116th Street and Amsterdam Avenue at two o'clock in the afternoon one Saturday. He warned me that I would really be sorry if I didn't bring the photos, and he told me not to have anybody with me, just to come alone. Well, with six FBI agents in a couple of cars watching me, I stood on the corner of 116th Street and Amsterdam with a large manila envelope.

Nothing happened for 30 minutes, but then two or three teenage guys came out of an apartment building on the other side of the street opposite me and looked around, then went back in. But the FBI agents decided to check on them and got one of them to talk.

"It was him. He was just sixteen years old, the one who had been writing me all the horrible letters that he had typed himself. I don't know what they did with him. I never heard. But a sixteen-year-old boy with a mind like that!"

This wasn't Bettie's only close call with a stalker in New York City. Another man, approximately 30 years old, who wore a black suit and black horn-rimmed glasses, stood across the street from her apartment for hours, looking up at her. He never approached the house, but it went on for weeks and weeks until he disappeared one day.

In late 1957 Bettie heard that her beloved apartment building was to be torn down to make way for a parking lot for Radio City Music Hall. "I even had a dream about it one night in which the buildings all along the street fell down and turned to rubble. They were going to tear it down the first of the year in 1958. And I didn't know where I would find another apartment as cheap as that one, where I could keep it when I went to Florida or to Nashville." Bettie looked for another place, but remained in a quandary about where to move.

That fall, Marvin Greene started to pester Bettie to marry him. Though she enjoyed Marvin's company and loved it when he announced his arrival at her apartment by singing "On the Street Where You Live" in his beautiful voice as he stood beneath her window, she turned down his proposal. "I didn't love Marvin enough to marry him. But I enjoyed being with him and could relax with him more than any man I ever knew. He was very sweet." His sudden desire to marry reminded her of the time many years before when a young Billy Neal goaded her into tying the knot before he shipped off to the Army.

Around this time the police knocked on Bettie's door with "pornographic pictures," nude photographs taken the night she had her only experience with alcohol. The cops explained that the shutterbug was in deep debt from betting on horses, so he had sold the illicit photographs. "He claimed he was ashamed of having to do such a thing, but if he didn't they [his debtors] would come after him," Bettie says. She had trusted the men in the camera clubs, and she was disappointed that the betrayal extended beyond getting her drunk and taking the photographs, to selling them for profit. "That was one thing that contributed to my leaving town."

In December 1957 Bettie decided to leave New York. "I was thirty-four years old, almost thirty-five. Even though everyone thought I was much younger, I was getting too old to do pin-ups." No one who worked with her knew her true age. "For years and years the magazines said I was twenty-two years old, and I never refuted it. Why should I tell them how old I was if I could get away with being younger? Besides, I had done enough modeling. The photographers had shot me so much, and there were so many pictures of me in circulation, I thought people would get sick of seeing me!"

Quietly and without any fanfare, Bettie Page went away. She called Paula Klaw to say that she was going to Florida and that she would write. She put her things in storage in New Jersey, said goodbye to her apartment and friends and left the city. She never returned to New York.

Life Goes On

1958 to 1978

Early in 1958 Tony Campo, just out of the service, walked briskly up Sixth Avenue on his way to pay a visit to his old friend Bettie Page. They corresponded occasionally while he was stationed in Japan, and Tony was anxious to hear news of her. He had important news of his own: He had brought a Japanese bride home with him. When Campo turned the corner onto West 46th, he looked in vain for Bettie's apartment. He checked to see if he had the right street. Something was definitely wrong. In place of the brownstone where Bettie lived stood a parking lot.

Opposite: Bettie on the beach in Florida, shortly after her retirement.

She had returned to Florida. Determined to leave her former career behind, she didn't contact any of the photographers. Instead, on a two-week vacation in Fort Lauderdale, she called her old boyfriend, Armond Walterson, who assured her that he was more than willing to resume their relationship. Bettie jumped on a bus to Key West, and he met her at the station. He was dating a pretty blond girl named Margaret, but he "dropped her like a hot potato" when Bettie came back on the scene. Margaret was so angry that she followed Bettie and Armond in her car, trying to rear-end them.

Armond, like Tony Campo, had a large, close-knit clan — the kind of family Bettie longed for as a child. "I was very fond of Armond's family. He had eleven brothers and sisters, and we would all go up to Boca Chica to the beach on picnics. His mother was just like a young girl. She would jump rope with us and have running sack races and things like that. She was a real card."

In early 1958 Bettie and Armond were playing volleyball on the beach when she reached for the ball and heard something crack in her back. She fell to the sand, paralyzed. Armond carried her to the hospital, where she learned that she had an acute sprain of the left joint of the sacrum. In agonizing pain and unable to work, she spent the next four months in a wheelchair. Spending all her savings on food and lodging, soon she couldn't afford to keep up the payments on her storage space in New Jersey. When the money ran out, Bettie lost all her belongings, including the bathing suits and dresses she made herself and childhood keepsakes. Moreover, she lost her entire collection of her own work. To this day, the subject of some of the world's most obsessive collecting owns virtually none of her own photographs and memorabilia.

After she recovered from the accident, Bettie taught fifth grade at Harris Elementary School in Key West, but it was a repeat of her former experience as a student teacher at Peabody College. A very disruptive student in the class, the son of a naval officer, held back year after year, proved to be Bettie's nemesis. He was already a teenager in a class of 10-year-olds. He caused Bettie problems with his own behavior, and by inciting his fellow students. Bettie lasted only one semester, deciding once and for all that she wasn't adept at controlling unruly boys.

On November 26, 1958, Bettie and Armond married at the First Methodist Church in downtown Key West, Florida, with Armond's large family in attendance. Bettie wore a manila-colored silk dress that she had made herself. Soon after the wedding, Bettie passed the civil service examination and began work as a secretary in the Department of Public Works in Key West. Armond worked as the head of shipping at the U.S. Naval Station. Although both had good jobs, they decided to collaborate on a business venture that would free them from office work. In 1959 each contributed $1,000 to purchase a fishing boat. Together, working on weekends and late into the evenings, they built 100 lobster traps, hand-painting the corks and bottles. Rising before sunrise to set the traps, they pulled up the nets late in the day after finishing their office jobs. They hoped to build a good business selling the lobsters to restaurants all through the Florida Keys, where they were in high demand. Unfortunately, a group of local youths sabotaged their plans by continually vandalizing their traps. At the end of their long workday, Bettie and Armond returned to find that they were left with only one or two lobsters — enough for dinner, but hardly enough to support a business. Discouraged, they sold the boat for $600, taking a big loss. "That was my only venture into private business," says Bettie.

She and Armond had only one fight in their entire relationship. On December 31, 1958, Bettie pleaded with him to take her dancing — her New Year's Eve ritual for many years — but he didn't want to go. She had tried to teach him to dance, but "he was a hopeless case. He had two left feet." Armond's refusal disappointed her. "I should never have married Armond. He was much too young for me," Bettie reflects. "I got bored to death because we just had three things in common: movies, sex and hamburgers. He was a fiend over hamburgers. That's all he wanted me to cook and all he ate when we out to dinner." In addition to the monotony of their lives, Bettie realized that he possessed none of her adventurous spirit. He liked to stay in Key West, content with the same routine day in and day out, whereas Bettie had a wide variety of interests and liked to try new things. It was particularly difficult for her that he was afraid to travel.

After Armond refused to go dancing on New Year's Eve, Bettie changed into slacks and a sweater and started to walk toward the beach. She intended to sit on the wall at the shore and look at the stars. "Suddenly, as if taken by the hand, I crossed the street. I looked up and there was a little white church with a white neon cross burning over the top. The doors were open and I heard singing. I was compelled to go in. I sat down in the back, and the minister started delivering a salvation sermon for my benefit, I know," she laughs. But the experience was a powerful one.

Bettie listened to the sermon, and by the end she concluded that the missing element in her life was a spiritual one. She continued to go to that church every Sunday, befriending a Sunday school teacher from Akron, Ohio, who took her out in her boat on weekends. From their discussions about the Good Book, Bettie's interest in Biblical studies was born. "I received the Lord Jesus Christ as my personal savior."

Ten months after she and Armond married, Bettie decided to go back to Nashville for a three-week visit to make some decisions about her life. She will never forget the tears in Armond's eyes as she got on the bus to go back home. Three weeks later he drove all the way to Nashville, but when he arrived unannounced at Edna Page's house, she gave him the bad news: He was too late. Bettie had just boarded the bus to California. Her brother Jimmie lived in the Los Angeles area and had encouraged her to come to California.

Bettie headed west. In Los Angeles she could enjoy the temperate weather and perennial sunshine she loved in Florida, plus the support of her closest brother. In Los Angeles she found an apartment at the edge of the Hollywood Hills on Vista del Mar near Hollywood Boulevard. As she perused the want ads in the *Los Angeles Times*, she saw that the First Methodist

Church downtown was looking for a secretary. She applied but didn't get the job. Walking away from the interview, she heard

Enjoying a quiet afternoon at the Palm Beach Amphitheatre.

gospel music coming from a loudspeaker above a little store. Two girls carrying books walked out of a building. "The strongest desire came over me to find out what that building was," Bettie says. "I started asking the girls questions about it. It was BIOLA, the Bible Institute of Los Angeles." At five o'clock the next morning Bettie woke up excited. She took a bus to La Mirada, where the Bible Institute was moving to merge with a Bible college. She had no money and no job, but the Institute advanced her tuition and money for room and board. She enrolled that day and began taking evening classes.

Bettie got a job as a secretary to the president of the Institute's radio station. She worked there for four months, but didn't earn enough money to continue with her Bible training. Then she went to work for the contracts administrator of Lockheed Aircraft International, which was just around the corner on Sixth Street. With money saved from that job, she enrolled in Moody Bible Institute in Chicago. There, from June 1961 until one year later, she attended summer school and evening classes while she worked for Compton's Encyclopedia as secretary to the educational research director.

Bettie spent one year in Chicago, living in a small apartment on LaSalle Street at the corner of Elm Street. She spent her spare time walking in Lincoln Park, on Oak Street Beach and along Michigan Avenue. Never a fan of cold weather, Bettie recalls

the awful flu she caught that winter, the coldest she'd ever experienced. She preferred summertime in the city, when she would lie in the sun along Lake Michigan. The highlight of her time in Chicago was working as a counselor for the Billy Graham Crusades. For 19 evenings in a row, she counseled women who were curious about Graham's message. She says the experience gave her much joy. When she left Chicago, Bettie attended a month-long Bible confer-

ence in Winona Lake, Indiana, where she heard lectures by the best Bible scholars in the country. The conference site was on the lake, where outdoor services were conducted in the early evening, while the sun set and dusky light shone through the pine trees. The beauty of the location drew her back for four consecutive summers.

Bettie spent her third year of Bible college at Multnomah School of the Bible in Portland, Oregon, "where it rained all the nine months I was there," laments the notorious sun-worshipper. "I had to carry an umbrella every day. But it was a good Bible school, and the plants and trees in Portland were huge and beautiful. I liked it there."

Bettie lived off campus in the home of one of the Bible school's former teachers, high in the hills above Portland. She enjoyed a splendid view of the city from her window. As part of her studies at Multnomah, Bettie worked at the Louise Home, where she counseled approximately 50 pregnant and unmarried teenagers; two were only 13 years old. Bettie enjoyed taking the girls to church and to the services she conducted with her friend and fellow Bible student, Sharon Reed.

Just as she was about to graduate, Bettie received a letter from her stepmother, Lulu Page, announcing that her father had to have a second leg amputated. Because of a severe case of diabetes undiagnosed for years, Roy Page had already lost one leg. "Like a fool, he would never go to a doctor for a checkup," Bettie remembers. Lulu told Bettie in her letter that Roy had begun to blame God for his health problems. Lulu wanted Bettie to come home and help him deal with his bitterness, and perhaps assist in bringing back his faith.

This wouldn't be the first time Roy Page experienced salvation. In the 1950s he had spent four years at Nazarene Bible College in Nashville. By the time he discovered he had diabetes, he had been a lay preacher for several years. Bettie declares that although her father was uneducated, he read the Bible with the understanding of a college professor. He wasn't intimidated by the difficult language of the King James version, and his comprehension and insight amazed Bettie. She believes his understanding of the Bible was truly inspired.

Bettie heard her father preach many times. He captivated his flock by admitting guilt for his previous sins and testifying that his faith had saved him. "He would get very emotional and cry while he was preaching," Bettie says. "He'd give his testimony about his sinful life. His conscience bothered him for years over the way he mistreated my mother and us children. He couldn't keep from crying when he delivered a sermon. I would sit in the audience feeling very sorry for him." Bettie doesn't doubt the sincerity of her father's reformation. "He was so repentant," Bettie says. Yet when Bettie confronted him in the presence of Lulu about the sexual abuse, he denied it. He denied it to his dying day.

Though he never admitted what he had done, Bettie was convinced of Roy's remorse and chose to forgive him for abandoning the children to poverty and for his sexual transgressions against her. Her religious convictions didn't allow her to harbor animosity. "You have to forgive someone who has received Jesus and has repented for his sins," she says, believing that forgiveness is the true message of Christianity.

In June 1963 Bettie hurried to Nashville. Roy was very ill and soon slipped into a coma. According to Lulu, he had exhibited the beginnings of dementia, imagining things that weren't really happening. He died in January 1964 at 68 years of age.

Back in Nashville Bettie began to teach Sunday school at a small mission operated by the First Baptist Church in the housing project in south Nashville. Her charges were 13-year-old girls. "They'd all pile in my old Ford station wagon with their mothers and we would go to Old Hickory Lake on picnics," she remembers with fondness. "It was a very happy time in my life. The best years of my life."

Inspired by her work with the girls, and by her good experience with the Billy Graham Crusades, Bettie discovered the true calling of her post-pin-up career. She wanted to spend the rest of her life doing missionary work. She applied to several missionary boards, but was rejected every time — not because she had been a pin-up model, but because she was divorced.

Bettie came up with a new plan: While working for Benson Printing Company, she applied for scholarships to finance graduate studies. She received an NDEA Educational Loan from the government because her father had been wounded in World War I. Returning to Peabody College full-time in the fall of 1963, she pursued a master's degree in english and journalism. Bettie says that of the many short stories she wrote in graduate school, the two best were about witnessing the voodoo rituals in Haiti and the failed lobster business with Armond. The stories have not survived.

In late 1963 Armond called Bettie. His new girlfriend was pregnant, and he asked Bettie to give him a divorce. She agreed, arranging for the papers through Armond's attorney in Key West, even paying for the proceedings herself.

Once again Bettie was single. During the three years she attended Bible colleges, her teachers and pastors suggested that if she could lead her first husband Billy Neal to religion, it would be God's will that they remarry. At the end of 1963, Bettie and Billy started seeing each other again and she taught him about the Bible. One day as they sat in his car looking out over Old Hickory Lake, he prayed to accept Jesus as his savior. Bettie believed Billy's intentions were sincere. She thought that her teachers were right: God intended her to bring him back to the church.

The two remarried. Billy had a nice home close to the Cumberland River, and Bettie moved in with him. But in spite of their shared religious beliefs, there was a new problem: They didn't consummate the marriage. Bettie claims that Billy got the notion that she had contracted a venereal disease in New York. He told her that he thought she was "unclean," and didn't want to have sex with her.

Between his marriages to Bettie, Billy had married and divorced another woman named Betty. "Good thing," Bettie remarks, "since he had a tattoo with my name on it." One month after Bettie and Billy remarried, Billy drove to Mississippi to pick up his daughter from his second marriage for a visit. When Billy and the six-year-old girl returned, Bettie announced that she wanted to go to a Bible lecture on the Book of Ephesians; earlier, she had heard the first part of the lecture and was curious to hear the rest.

"You're not going anywhere," Billy replied. Bettie thought she had covered herself by preparing a nice dinner for Billy and his daughter, and didn't understand his reaction. But he repeated, "You're going to stay here and entertain my daughter." She protested, but he threw her on the floor and grabbed her by the throat, choking her in front of the child. Gasping for breath, Bettie tried to fight him off. Her only thought was that she didn't want to die. "I was about to pass out and could hardly breathe, when finally I was able to say, 'Billy, if you kill me, God will punish you for eternity.' It must have frightened him, because he stopped choking me and got up."

Terrified and angry, Bettie stayed in the house, but had thoughts of killing Billy during the night. She couldn't believe what he had done to her — especially in front of a small child. "I imagine that was traumatic for that child all her life," Bettie says. In the morning she called her brother Jack, who helped her pack her belongings and drove her away. Because they hadn't consummated the marriage, Bettie was able to procure an annulment, and this was her last encounter with Billy. But even after the last violent incident, Bettie felt remorse about not being able to make it work. "I had a terrible time giving up on that marriage. I didn't want to be like my parents." Yet she says she doesn't have any bitterness toward him. "But," she declares with finality, "I never want to see him again."

After the breakup with Billy, Bettie continued to study diligently at Peabody. With almost all the requirements for her master's degree completed, she decided to take a year off to go to Florida. She wanted to see the ocean again and take a course in historical research at the University of Miami.

Every week Bettie went dancing at the Palace Ballroom on Biscayne Boulevard, where an American band and a Latin band played. On an August evening in 1965 she spotted a handsome man about her age smiling at her. Though she liked his looks immediately, she could tell that he was shy. Bettie asked him to dance, but he declared that he didn't know how. "Finally I pulled him up on his feet. He wasn't a bad dancer at all! They were playing Frank Sinatra's song 'Strangers in the Night' and that became our theme song." Six months later, on Valentine's Day 1967, Bettie married her third husband, Harry Lear.

Harry was a divorced father and the custodial parent of three children between the ages of seven and eleven. The courtship was fast and romantic, and all the pieces of a successful marriage seemed to fall into place. They became lovers right away. Harry was willing to accept Bettie's religion, and to embrace it as his own. Bettie and the children got along. "I always regretted that I didn't have children of my own. I wanted two boys and a girl, and I had that with Harry's children." The new family attended church together on Sundays and traveled together, taking camping trips, going to the beach and going bowling. Bettie believed she finally had the family she'd dreamed of all her life.

Soon, however, the children began to resent Bettie's presence in the house, yearning for their own mother. Though she had given up custody, she made the children feel that by loving Bettie, they were betraying her. Her campaign to cause Harry trouble in his new marriage extended to harassing Bettie. "She would telephone us in the middle of the night and tell me to go to hell. She would never let me talk to her about the problems we were having with the children." According to Bettie, Lear's children would sit for hours on visitation weekends waiting for their mother, who wouldn't always show up. Sometimes she wouldn't even telephone. Nothing was more upsetting to Bettie than seeing children suffer, reminding her of the troubles in her own youth. Yet there was little she could do. "The poor little things would sit there waiting for her very patiently, not seeming to mind how she treated them. They still loved her very much."

After five years of trying to get Harry's children to accept her, Bettie gave up on the marriage. They divorced in January 1972, but because they were still such good friends, she moved into Harry's spare bedroom. Never conventional, this new situation suited the enigmatic Bettie. She lived in Lear's house until 1978.

Not eager to resume office work, she became interested in tropical plants and bought every book she could find on the subject. Harry had a very large backyard in which she had plenty of room to experiment. Bettie planted a wide variety of palm trees and fruit trees. "But my pride and joy was a free-form pear-shaped pool, which I learned to build from a book." Bettie dug the hole herself and made the wooden forms for pouring the concrete. Then disaster struck. About a dozen tree frogs "came from nowhere, congregating in the water and in the trees. They squawked all night long and we couldn't sleep. Then the females laid hundreds of tiny black eggs and in no time at all, the water was full of tadpoles." Soon Bettie had to drain the pool. But she would still go into the dry pool during the day, and sit on the seat and read. "I was very proud of my beautiful oasis. It was the only thing I ever created."

In October 1978 Bettie moved back to California. Her brother Jimmie was divorced and terribly lonely. He wrote to Bettie for months, asking her to come and stay with him. She lived with Jimmie for nine years, helping him take care of his house in Lawndale, completely unaware that a few miles up the freeway in Los Angeles, the Bettie Page revival had begun.

"That I may know Him, and the power of His resurrection, and the fellowship of His sufferings, being made conformable unto His death."

Bettie's picture and favorite verse from the 1963 Multnomah Bible School Annual.

PART III

Cult Icon

THE NATION'S NEWSPAPER
USA TODAY
NO. 1 IN THE USA... FIRST IN DAILY READERS

THE LEGEND OF BETTY PAGE

BETTY PAGES

SUCCESSFUL SIREN: Betty Page's fame in the 1950s is still followed today, as evidenced by magazine The Betty Pages. 'Rocketeer,' a Disney film with a Betty-based heroine, opens June 21.

COVER STORY

Prozac maker offers doctors legal help
By Mike Snider
USA TODAY

Pin-up star has leg up on naughtiness

The Gay Rights Protests { Robin Podolsky covers the demos
Doug Sadowski examines the initiative

LA WEEKLY FREE

IN SEARCH OF BETTIE PAGE
BY KAREN ESSEX

HOW A '50s PINUP BECAME A '90s MYTH

PLUS Miles Davis Remembered

THE CASE OF The VANISHING Pinup

ALTHOUGH MODEL BETTIE PAGE DISAPPEARED MYSTERIOUSLY NEARLY THIRTY YEARS AGO, FOR HER GROWING CULT OF ADMIRERS, LOVE STILL HURTS

by I. S. LEVINE

Betty Page Talks Sin: A Lecture/Demonstration ©

A NOSTALGIC LOOK AT
BETTIE PAGE

VOLUME 4 NUMBER 4

The Queen of Pin-ups, whose career spanned the hey-day of that art form, pictured in all her magnificent beauty!

$5.00

AN EROS GOLDSTRIPE SPECIAL

The Revival Begins

Bettie Page disappeared from the public eye but the public did not forget. To the core group of her cultists, she remained the ineluctable sex icon of their own imaginations — and the pin-up model of the century. During her exile years, Bettie Page was never out of vogue. Her most devoted fans kept her image alive from the day she disappeared.

Throughout the end of the 1950s and into the 1960s, men's magazines continued to print her pictures and run articles featuring her, as if she had granted a recent interview and was still actively modeling. She also remained in the *Movie Star News* catalogues, where Paula Klaw continued to receive orders for her photographs. In the ensuing decades, fervently, collectors and fans continued to accumulate her photographs and memorabilia. Then, several publications acknowledged that she had disappeared and published retrospectives on her, such as *Bound Beauties of Irving Klaw, A Nostalgic Look at Bettie Page* and, from 1978 to 1980, four editions of *Private Peeks*. By this time, the mystery of her whereabouts began to fuel the fascination with her image.

As awareness of Bettie Page spread, she became a pop culture icon, celebrated with merchandise, fanzines and artwork in tribute to her. In the 1980s and early 1990s, the national media launched an extensive, unsuccessful search for her. Suddenly, Bettie Page, once a well-kept underground cult secret, had become an international phenomenon.

"She was the best thing to come out of the Fifties besides Marilyn Monroe," says J. B. Rund, who initiated the Bettie Page publishing revival with four editions of *Private Peeks*. "I tried to present them as historical documents, a chronicle of that period. And I tried to present the whole of Bettie Page — as homogenous and universal a portrait of her as possible. But she's many different things to many different people."

A kaleidoscopic Bettie by airbrush artist Marc Greenblum.

Mikal Gilmore, Pop Culture Critic and Author: "Bettie Page might be the greatest nude model of the century, though the term nude undersells what makes her so riveting, so genuinely sexy: the flawless and natural perfection of her expression from photo to photo, from year to year. I've never seen a single shot of her that seemed forced or fake. Or non-electric. Whether the session was meant to be funny, scary or feral hardly mattered. Bettie meets the camera on her own terms. She looks confident, smart, good-humored and ultimately in control. Every picture of Bettie Page can prove an erotic experience: her aplomb, her carriage, invite and play with you, her eyes enthrall you. And you know that no matter how much you stare or dream or pray, you could never get enough of what it is that her face and body seem to promise. That's what makes her a love for all time, and that's what makes her art indelible."

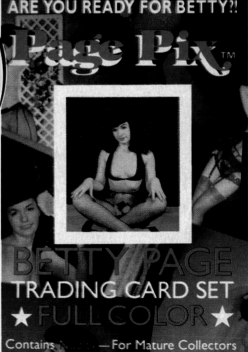

Herb Lichtenstein, Playwright/Director, *Betty Page Talks Sin: A Lecture/Demonstration*: "If physical beauty were all that Bettie possessed, then she would be just another in the legion of pretty models. It was her inner beauty shining through that dazzled us and set her apart from the pack. What impresses me is her accessibility. She stands exactly halfway between the glacial *Vogue* model — who projects a 'Don't come near me' vibe — and the voracious Jayne Mansfield type who screams, 'get over here and I'll eat you alive.' Bettie exuded amiability, friendliness. She didn't want to be worshipped. She wanted you to buy a cherry Coke with two straws." Right: Shel-Tone Publications has released the classic Bettie in 3-D slides as a set of trading cards.

236

Bettie is flattered that she has so many fans in the pop music world. "*Aerosmith* likes me? I'm thrilled, but I don't pretend to understand it. It's most unusual. Don't they know how old I am?" Recently, a young booking agent inquired if Bettie would host the annual summer alternative music tour, Lollapalooza. Bettie's reply: "My heavens no! But isn't it sweet of them to ask." Right: The 1995 and 1996 Bettie Page calendars. Far right: In 1995 noted artist Clayburn Moore created a beautiful bronze sculpture of Bettie in a limited edition of 50 copies.

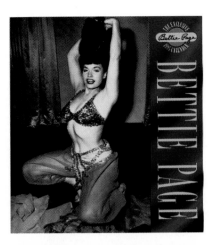

Rock and roll icon: "She's *the end*," says Chuck Mead of Arista recording artists BR5-49. "Bettie took all the degradation and evil out of whatever she did. She made everything seem like it was innocent and fun. That smile, those eyes. They're eternal." Raul Malo, lead singer of the Mavericks, says, "Bettie Page is a *woman*. She looks like a woman. She moves like a woman. There's no mistake about what she is. And that's why very young men still love her." Adds lead guitar player Nick Kane: "Bettie Page represents a sense of daring and an individualism to young kids who are dedicated to living an authentic alternative lifestyle. To them, she's an inspiration and an icon. It's her look — so sultry and provocative. Go to any rockabilly show anywhere — Japan, Europe — and the Bettie Page look-a-like girls will be lined up from wall to wall. She's their hero."

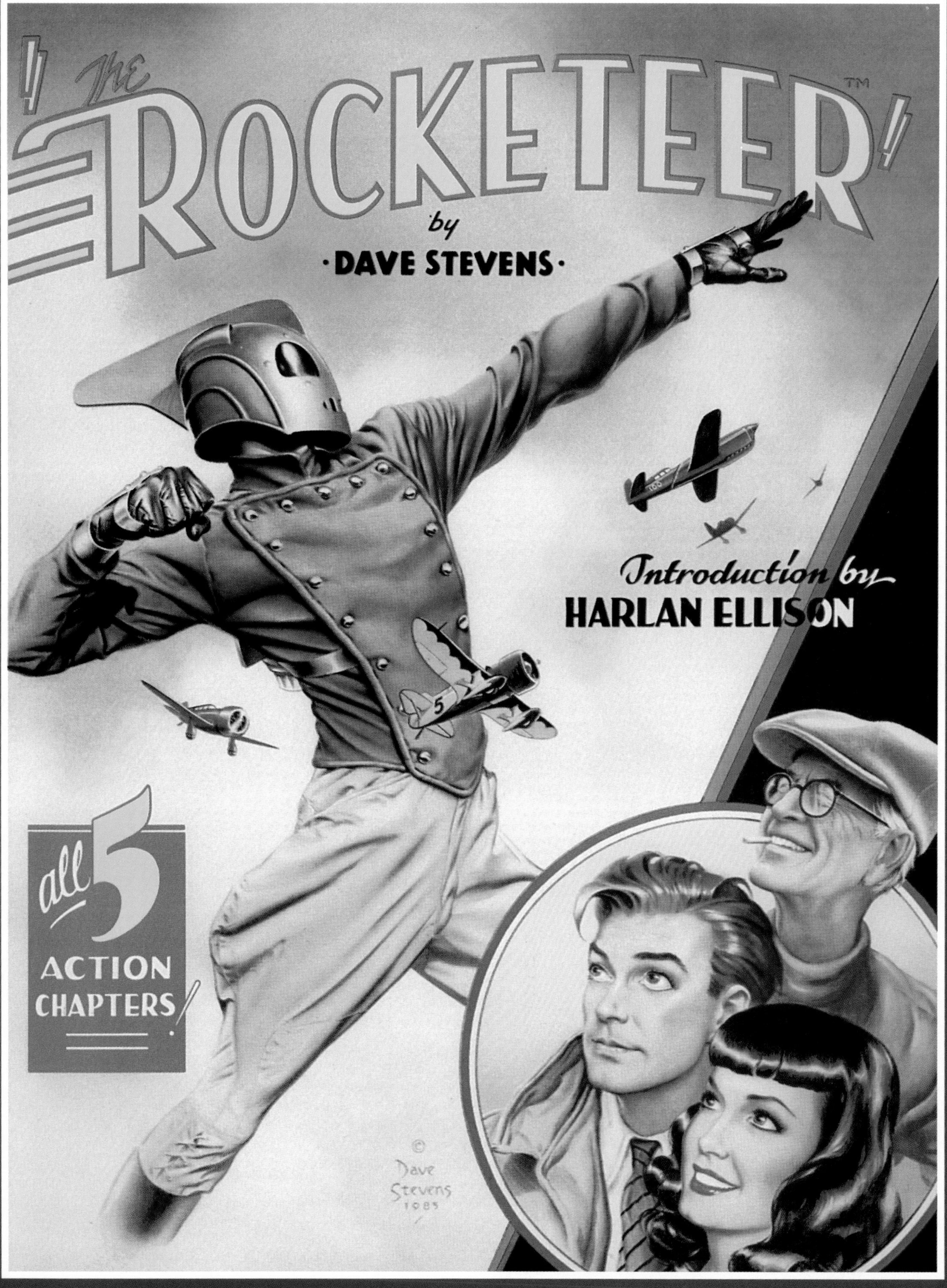

The ROCKETEER™
by
·DAVE STEVENS·
Introduction by
HARLAN ELLISON
all 5 ACTION CHAPTERS!
© Dave Stevens 1985

The Muse: Art and Comics

In 1976 Naomi Caryl, Bettie's friend from Sea Cliff Summer Theatre, attended the opening of a controversial show at a Los Angeles gallery. A young artist, Robert Blue, had painted huge canvases of women bound and gagged, and in other fetish scenarios; it was the talk of the town. Caryl regarded the enormous and shocking oils. Staring back at her, larger than life, was a face she hadn't seen in twenty-three years — that mysterious summer apprentice, Bettie Page.

Blue wasn't the only artist to honor Bettie. Artists world-wide recognized her iconic power and began to revive her image. As artists' muse, Bettie's star rose in conjunction with the looser, post-sexual revolution mores, and with the punk movement, which resurrected outsider imagery and dark iconography: skulls, gothic crosses and demons invoking sacrilege, and leather, spikes and chains invoking sexual deviance. Bettie Page, an underground fetish goddess, emerged as the perfect sex icon.

In addition to Blue, the foremost contemporary artists to paint Bettie Page include Dave Stevens and Olivia. While many painters, sculptors, photographers and comics artists continue to celebrate her image, Blue, Stevens and Olivia explore strikingly different aspects of her enduring appeal.

Facing page: Dave Stevens' *The Rocketeer* appeared in 1981 and featured a Bettie look-alike as the hero's girlfriend. The serial was credited with kick-starting the Page craze, stateside. Meanwhile, across the Atlantic, French artist Denis Sire styled his own tribute to Bettie (pictured above) in his 1981 series, *Bois Willys*. Curiously, neither artist was aware of the other's effort until both books were published.

A Model Spank with Bettie Page

Robert Blue

In the early 1970s a young artist, Robert Blue, decided it was time to take Bettie Page from the clandestine corner of Dad's private drawer and expose her exhilarating sexuality to the mainstream. Blue was probably Bettie's youngest fan in the 1950s. Thanks to an unorthodox childhood, he found her when he was in early adolescence. Robert's father was Ben Blue, the legendary comedian who socialized with W. C. Fields, ran a nightclub in Santa Monica and opened the Las Vegas Flamingo for Bugsy Siegel. His mother was a former showgirl and artist. Ben Blue and his circle of friends exposed Robert to their larger-than-life ways — and to their favorite reading matter. By the time he was seven years old, Blue exhibited a talent for paint-

Banana Leaf

ing. A few years later he began to collect men's fetish magazines from the 1950s, specifically *Exotique*, looking for things to paint. There he discovered Bettie Page — the whip-snapping, black-haired, corseted woman who became his muse. "The photography had an edge to it that contemporary art is always looking for — somewhere between myth and magic. It was electrically charged, especially to me at that age." Blue responded intuitively to Bettie and to the forbidden world of corsets, stockings, whips, catfights and high heels. "Discovering Bettie Page was discovering the dark side I had no idea even existed."

By the time Blue graduated from the Chouinard Institute (later Cal Arts) and served in the Vietnam War, it was a new era and Bettie's reign as America's pin-up queen was over. But Blue could not forget her and the images had so electrified him as a teen. "It was ironic. Bettie Page was a pivotal figure in the opening up of sexual freedom. The revolution of the 1960s grew from the seeds that she and other pioneers sowed the decade before. But the generation whose liberation she helped make possible had forgotten her. I had to do something. I started a painting."

Wagon Wheel

A Model Spank

are gonna love 'em.'"

Blue finished one painting and then began another. His one-canvas tribute soon became an obsession. When he completed 10 canvases, he brought transparencies of the paintings to Nicholas Wilder, then a premier contemporary art dealer in Los Angeles, but he was told that he had to wait eight months for an appointment. Blue waited outside the gallery until the receptionist was gone. Then he sneaked back into the gallery and introduced himself to Wilder, insisting that he review the slides. "He was cornered. He took them into the other room, and when he came out, he said, 'Robert, I hate these paintings. But I know a lot of people in New York who

Blue's New York and Los Angeles shows were successful; the paintings were sold to important American and European collectors. Blue intended to expand the series to 25 large-scale pieces that explored the sexual, cultural and psychological meaning of Bettie Page. However, he ran into two problems. The growing women's movement of the 1970s accused him of exploiting women because his paintings were "erotically incorrect." Moreover, he had heard from a source — later proved unreliable — that Bettie herself did not want him to paint her anymore. Blue would have stood his ground against the feminists' accusations. He believes his work is a meditation on sex and voyeurism, having nothing to do with the oppression of women. But he would not violate the wishes of his muse. Out of respect for Bettie, he stopped painting her, even while others capitalized during the 1980s on the trend he initiated.

Though he stopped painting her, Blue's

Lace

existing Bettie Page paintings retained their notoriety and continued to attract attention for the artist and for his muse, whose renown had yet to crest. Blue became a legend in his own right. Throughout the 1970s and 1980s, he received letters from Gay Talese, who sought Bettie for participation in his book *Thy Neighbor's Wife*, and others who were in search of the lost pin-up icon. In 1985 the movie *Heartbreakers* was released. Starring Peter Coyote as an artist obsessed with erotic and fetishist imagery, the film was modeled on Blue's life and featured his art.

In 1993 Bettie stunned her fans — Blue among them — by ending her long silence. After she reviewed for the first time some of

Red Ball Gag

Bettie Page in Bondage #5

Fishnet

the artwork she inspired, Bettie wrote him a letter informing him that the earlier message he received from her was false. She liked the paintings, and she invited him to continue the series. With Bettie's blessing, he has finally published six of his favorite vintage and two new paintings in limited editions of 150 prints. Today Blue believes the image of Bettie Page is more relevant and powerful than ever. "Her influence is everywhere. To find Madonna's source material, look at Bettie in her prime. To understand contem-porary fashion, observe what Bettie wore forty years ago. To know why Bettie Page symbol-izes sexual liberation and feminine power, uncover the subtext of her fetish photos and film."

Blue plans to complete the 25 painting Bettie Page series by 1997. At that time, he will exhibit them together in a one-time-only show, where visitors can witness the fruits of his lifelong obsession, and enter his private fetish world where Bettie Page reigns forever as its queen.

Dave Stevens

In the 1980s no one was more responsible than Dave Stevens, the evangelist behind the Bettie Page revival, for transforming the 1950s cult model into a contemporary pop culture icon. There is something about the discovery of Bettie Page in one's youth that etches her image indelibly into the mind. In his teens, while thumbing through a stack of vintage men's magazines, Stevens came upon a shot of Bettie in a bikini, standing ankle deep in water. "It stopped me cold. It took my breath away." He began to sketch his new obsession.

In the late 1970s Stevens saw an ad for 8mm loops of Bettie Page. He ordered a dozen of the tiny films from Movie Star News. He bought a Keystone projector and set it up in his office at Hanna-Barbera, where he worked as an artist and animator. Because they were silent, he added a Cab Calloway soundtrack — the perfect jazz accompaniment to Bettie's "wiggling." At lunchtime, he played the five five-minute films to what became a standing room only crowd. "We would hoot and holler. It was really fun," he recalls. When he left Hanna-Barbera, friends called him to ask if they could come to his new studio at lunch time to watch Bettie Page dance. He complied, dragging out the old projector at their request. He observed the effect his private infatuation had on others.

Opposite page: 1994 marked the surprise return of "Betty" to the *Rocketeer* series. Above: An emblematic image (circa, 1984) of the creation that launched one career and revived another. *The Rocketeer* was considered an instant classic by both comic book afficionados and pin-up fans everywhere.

WOW!

WH-WHAT'S THE MEANING OF THIS? WHO ARE YOU??

NO, I'D LOVE TO CLIFF, BUT I'M...GOING TO BE TIED UP THIS AFTERNOON!

DON'T TELL ME-- MORE "ART-PHOTOS"?

CLIFF, DON'T--WE'VE BEEN ALL THROUGH THAT!

WHY DON'T YOU CALL ME BACK TONIGHT? OKAY?

I'LL THINK ABOUT IT.

HMM...I'D HOPED TO POSTPONE THIS TRIP, UNTIL I'D DECIDED WHAT TO DO ABOUT CLIFF! I'LL JUST HAVE TO TELL HIM I'M VISITING AN AUNT! HE'LL PUT UP A FUSS...

IT'S THAT DANGEROUS?

YEA--!

...BUT I CAN'T LET HIM FIND OUT ABOUT MARCO! OH, WHY DID THIS HAVE TO GET SO COMPLICATED FOR ME?!

...JUST BECAUSE I'M A FEMALE...

"THE KIND MEN LIKE!" HMPH!

SORRY-- I CAME AS FAST AS I COULD!

WHERE'S CLIFF?

I'LL BE COUNTING ON YOU, HONEY! DON'T GET CRAZY...

AAAH... DON'T WORRY! I'LL DO THE RIGHT THING!

The creation that launched Stevens' career and the Bettie Page revival began inauspiciously. In 1982 a small comic press with some extra space in a forthcoming book invited him to come up with some quick "filler pages." He sketched several ideas, but, owing to his meticulous and perfectionist nature, he hated them all. Frustrated, he stopped drawing and secluded himself. He began to imagine a story that would combine all of his boyhood fantasies: nostalgia for a lost era, heroes, adventure, a man with a rocket who could fly — and a raven-haired girl named Bettie. He returned to the studio and drew it quickly, scripting the story and calling it *The Rocketeer*. He immortalized Bettie as the hero's girlfriend in the comic — his first for publication — which became an unexpected sensation. *The Village Voice* called it "the greatest comic book in the world." Harlan Ellison said "for all the hopeful attempts at doing a period comic book, only *The Rocketeer* captures the feel of those days. The artwork is modern, yet it has a tone of the twenties and thirties." More chapters of the book followed. Then, nine years after the story's modest debut as a "filler" strip, the *Rocketeer* phenomenon climaxed with the release of a Disney motion picture that grossed over $100 million world wide.

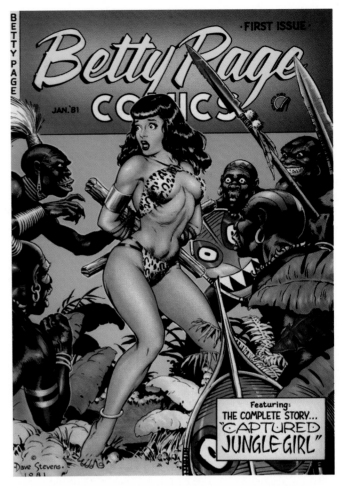

With *The Rocketeer* and through a series of pin-up paintings, Stevens introduced Bettie to a new generation of fans, mainly comics readers and collectors, and contemporary pin-up fans. *The Rocketeer* made Bettie the most popular comic book heroine of all time based on a real person. Tony Campo, a longtime comics collector, was in a large comic book store in New York City when he mentioned to a clerk that he'd dated Bettie Page. "I became a celebrity in the store," he says. "I had a hard time going back there once they found out."

Dave Stevens believes this adulation of Bettie is because she is the classic, genuine American Beauty. "She has an indescribable quality that separates her from all the other models of that time. You get a sense

Cover illustration for Italy's *Glamour* magazine, 1986. Above: Stevens satirized 1950's "Jungle Comics" with this apocryphal cover in 1980.

of pure joy from her, as though she just came alive for the camera and gave it her all. There's a timeless quality about her that gives her images a real currency even though they were shot some forty years ago. It's an amazing feat, to be able to bridge time the way she does. She is embraced by both sexes, and she's become a role model for young women — a maverick who did as she pleased without concern for the social restrictions of the time. Bettie was bold and independent when women just weren't allowed to be that. That's an admirable, risky quality that can invite trouble. Her image will still be around long after we're gone."

Stevens helped ensure that when he immortalized her as Cliff Secord's girlfriend in *The Rocketeer*. Ironically, it was the success of Stevens's own comic that caused him to stop painting his idol. The Page craze he had set in motion introduced her to a new generation of faithful fans who loved her, but it also attracted speculators and opportunists. Stevens decided to distance himself from his own creation. "The Bettie Page exploitation movement had set in and merchandise, most of it second rate, was suddenly being generated by scores of artists and publishers who cared nothing about her. They were after the quick buck. It got totally out of control, and I wanted no part of it." Stevens vowed to never draw her again without her blessing and without sharing any bounty to be had from using her image. He did not make the decision easily; she had disappeared in the 1950s and he feared she would never be heard from again.

Late in 1992 Dave Stevens heard a rumor that Bettie was to be featured on *Lifestyles of the Rich and Famous*. When the show aired,

Painted in 1983, "Betty's Bath" was Stevens's first attempt at emulating the Vargas style. Opposite page: Centerfold from *Bettie Page Comics #1*.

he sat mesmerized, listening to a voice he never thought he would hear, the voice of Bettie Page. Like Robert Blue, Stevens wanted no part of exploiting Bettie, particularly if she was alive and well. While some who had used her image fled for the hills to avoid any obligation to share the profits they earned from exploiting her, and even disputed her right to protect her own name and image, Stevens sought out the Page family and asked how he could help. Stevens then got to fulfill a 20 year obsession. He had the privilege of meeting Bettie and showing her *The Rocketeer* for the first time. When she revealed that she had never seen the movie and that she was about to watch it on network television, long-time fan Hugh Hefner hosted a private screening for her, Stevens, and a small group of friends.

Bettie inspired Stevens to publish a new chapter, featuring her character's return to the comic. Currently he is hard at work generating new projects for her, from which she will receive a substantial portion of the profits. He's begun a new anthology, *Bettie Page Comics*, and a sculpture co-designed with Kent Melton. He is also completing an oil painting that he says will be the best Bettie image he's ever done. Most gratifying of all, he entered her very small circle of friends. "She's a remarkable woman: articulate, well read, with a really sweet sense of humor. She's everything I thought she would be. And best of all, I can finally look her in the eye and say 'thank you.'"

Olivia

If Robert Blue celebrated Bettie's image as the dark fetish queen and Dave Stevens exalted her as the girl-next-door, Olivia De Barardinis, the woman who paints with a direct pipeline to male fantasies, translated both of those aspects into bewitching fantasy-erotica. Known by her first name only, Olivia is a petite, soft-spoken woman — an unlikely candidate to be one of the most successful, skillful and well-known contemporary erotic artists in the world. Olivia's paintings, and the prints, calendars and greeting cards of her art, are popular worldwide. Important collectors of erotic art from many countries anxiously await her new creations, gathering at her openings to see the latest collection of her often chimerical interpretations of female beauty. For years Olivia's favorite and most popular model has been Bettie Page. "I have never understood why she didn't get the attention she deserved in her own time," Olivia says. "She was the dark-haired Monroe. I'm just glad she's getting it now."

Olivia has painted Bettie for over a decade, and continues to do so. Through *Playboy* and other avenues she meets a stream of women who want to model — an endless supply of perfectly proportioned

female flesh. Yet, she continues to put paintings of a 1950s icon on the covers of her yearly calendars and her greeting cards. "Bettie has so much life, and it shows in the photos of her. A lot of people assume they

BETTIE PAGE

can model, but when they get in front of the camera, they can't move. We see breathtaking women all the time in magazines and on television, but they can't get this kind of magic across. Bettie could carry it all off. She could parade around in impossible high heels. She could play the dominant or the submissive and always look like she was having a ball. She took the edge off the gravity of these sexual situations by the look on her face. And that was remarkable."

Olivia also stresses that Bettie was an original. "My models now have the entire history of glamour modeling to draw on and add to, but who were Bettie's role models? Much of the time, she wasn't even being shot by professionals. No Helmut Newton or Herb Ritts was shooting her. And yet…I can only think she spent lots of time in front of the mirror. When I'm painting her, I am always amazed. If you tear down her features, you realize that she wasn't perfect. Somehow, though, it all works. Imperfection can be so much more interesting than perfection."

BETTIE PAGE

Eric Stanton

Artist Eric Stanton hasn't seen Bettie since 1957, but she still inspires his work. "Of course I fell in love with Bettie, but who didn't?

Let's face it: she was the greatest." Stanton had a studio at the corner of 43rd Street and Eigth Avenue during the 1950s. He worked for the Klaws from 1948-1960, creating pen-and-ink drawings and watercolor and gouache paintings of fantasy scenarios for at least 20 Klaw publications, including *Pleasure Bound, Bound in Leather, Fighting Femmes* and *Battling Women*. Stanton's studio was raided in the late 1950s. In an attempt to coerce him into testifying against a publisher for whom he worked, the authorities took every piece of his own artwork and his entire collection of the work of others. Stanton refused to incrimate his boss, and when he asked for his artwork back, he was told that it had been destroyed.

Two panels from Eric Stanton's *Sweeter Gwen*, a book length serial produced in the late 1950s.

In Vogue
Fashion and Style

In the 1950s, not one fashion magazine dared publish a picture of Bettie Page. Today, she influences fashion and style around the world. Supermodels look to her for inspiration, designers send down the runway the clothes she pioneered and photographers recall her look and attitude. In the world of fashion Bettie Page will never go out of style.

Body di pelle, Swish.
Collant Ibici; scarpe
Vivienne Westwood.
Nella pagina accanto.
Pull con cintura e
pantaloncini,
Blumarine. Scarpe
Fornarina.

"2" />

PIN★UP

Pelle, voile, stampe e pois. Ma anche
abiti e tailleur neri. Per un nuovo
charme ispirazione anni cinquanta.

Vanity Fair called her our "Über-pin-up" and in the *New York Times* William Grimes wrote that "almost 40 years after she withdrew into obscurity, her star shines more brightly than it ever did in her brief heyday from 1951 to 1957." Grimes proclaimed that of the hundreds of models from that era, "only Bettie Page lives on." That popularity led to a look-alike phenomenon.

Tendenze

A cura di Drory Burstin

Pulp Fiction

Intrigo, mistero, perico-lo, suspence... ma an-che amore, eccitazione, avventura. Ecco cosa compravano ogni mese milioni di americani per un prezzo che andava dai cinque cents al quarto di dollaro, negli anni Trenta e Quaranta. *Pulp fiction*, ov-vero piccole grandi storie fittamente stampate su carta scadente, dalle co-pertine coloratissime che già riassumevano nell'im-magine il contenuto, per lo più torbido, della pub-blicazione. Letture "facili da consumare e altrettanto facili da dimenticare", ve-re e proprie macchine del sogno, economiche fughe dalla routine quotidiana. Ed è a questo genere che si è ispirato Quentin Taranti-no per il suo film, Palma d'oro a Cannes e ora can-didato all'Oscar, un noir a tinte forti impressionante e grottesco. E il repêchage ha contagiato anche la moda. Smalto e rossetto rosso fuoco, lingerie ne-ra, e tacchi vertiginosi, ec-co una donna forte, ag-gressiva e sensuale che non esita a esibire il reggise-no per ottenere ciò che vuole. Passando così dalla *pulp fiction* alla *pulp fashion*.

In questa pagina, in alto, alcune co-pertine di "pulp" originali ameri-cani, tratte dal libro "Danger is my business" (Lee Server, Chronicle Books). Qui accanto, Uma Thurman in una sequenza di "Pulp Fiction" di Quentin Tarantino (Photo Moviel

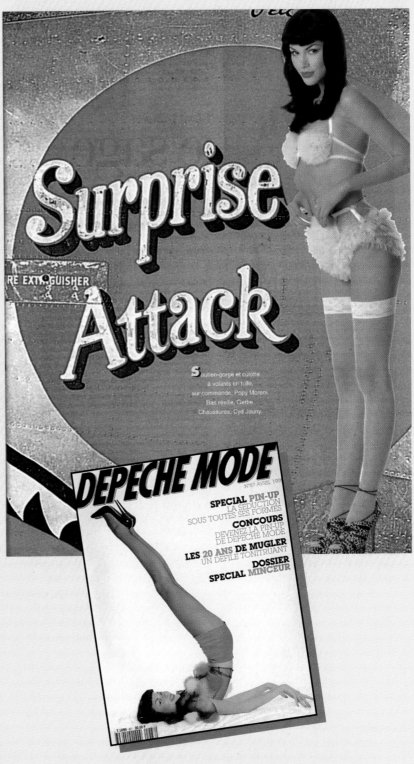

DEPECHE MODE N°87 AVRIL 199

SPECIAL PIN-UP
LA SEDUCTION
SOUS TOUTES SES FORMES

CONCOURS
DEVENEZ LA PIN-UP
DE DEPECHE MODE

LES 20 ANS DE MUGLER
UN DEFILE TONITRUANT

DOSSIER
SPECIAL MINCEUR

In the 1990s fashion magazines from around the world — including France, Germany, Spain, Italy and England — published look-alike tributes that credited Bettie Page for defining her era, for reviving the pin-up style in fashion today and even for inspiring the "Pulp Fiction" look.

The contents of Bettie Page's private closet — whips, riding crops, corsets, garter belts, stockings, boots, sheer black fabrics, leopard prints, gloves, halters, leather and rubber garments of all kinds — have gone public on the runways of Paris, Milan, London and New York. Long before Versace, Gaultier, Dolce & Gabbana, Westwood, Blumarine and others, Bettie glorified fetish, seduction and voyeurism, anticipating the day they would become fashion. Her contribution to modern style climaxed in Paris when John Galliano used her image to signal the return of seductive glamour.

Runway photos courtesy Randy Brooke.

Elizabeth Snead: Fashion Editor, *USA Today*. "Just what makes Bettie Page so special? It's not the costumes, the girlie-girl poses, the ball-gags and stiletto heels. It's the eyes. Something unmistakable in Bettie's eyes. Call it a spark. Call it intelligence, irony; an obvious sense of the absurd. An innocent sensuality. Self confidence. Whatever. Something's there. Unlike most pin-up models of her day who gazed dully into the glazed distance, Bettie looked straight into the lens as if she was letting you in on a cosmic joke. Even when she was tied up, her eyes snickered that she could get out. If she really wanted to. You can almost hear her chuckling between the shots. I've covered fashion trends and models for two decades, and I've never seen the impish glee in Bettie's eyes in any other model. And I'll bet it's still there. Don't take my word for it. Stare long enough at a Bettie pin-up and tell me if, every so often, out of the corner of your eye, you don't catch her winking."

Albert Watson, photographer: "She's the perfect combination of sensuality and sexuality. Bettie Page always looks modern. Like Elvis, James Dean and Montgomery Clift, Bettie Page brought something modern to the Fifties. She is 'Fifties' only because she happened to live then. There is a strange kind of modernity in the way she presented herself — the hair, the makeup, the way that she posed and worked the body. Bettie Page is more modern than Marilyn Monroe or Jayne Mansfield. She doesn't look dated.

You could do her shots now, exactly the same. I perceive her as a very strong persona. There is such a definite thing in her aura and her way of being that I think I would have been tempted to photograph her exactly as she was. She also had such good taste. Even though many of the things she did were fringe, she never exhibited bad taste. She was never cheap. She may have appeared in cheap magazines, on cheap postcards, or was shot by some bad photographers, but she always rose above that. Seventy or eighty percent of her photographs, you could run in *Vogue*. I'm sure she must have dominated the photographers, because she has too clear an identity. She is always Bettie Page. She always held on to the essence of who she was. That's why her appeal is not nostalgic, it's classic."

Chantal Thomass
Fashion Designer

"Bettie Page was very modern for the Fifties. She did many things that in the period were very shocking. She was *très liberée*, modern, never *démodée*. In that repressed era for women, Bettie Page seemed to have the upper hand because she expressed and enjoyed her sexuality. She was not straight-laced or a stuffed shirt.

She is even more popular today because she has a modern face — the hair, the make-up, the attitude. It's the same when you see a picture of Chanel from 1930 — it could have been taken today. Some other stars from that period really look dated, but Bettie's make-up is not excessive. It never seems vulgar like some of the others. She wasn't the most beautiful but she was the most memorable — fresh and natural.

She seemed very free. She wanted to give pleasure and amuse, and you can see in her face that she did it for fun. Even when she looks submissive, Bettie gives me the idea that 'I want to do it. I'm free.' She does it as if it were a game. I am influenced by the pin-up look, but very often I try to be careful because some people don't understand. I know I cannot put certain clothes on the runway because people in fashion would accuse me of making a woman into an object.

The pin-up look is popular again because people need beauty. Now all the models are very sexy. It is part of the lot of a woman to be seductive. And it has been forgotten for many years. Women forgot to be women. We can have both. We can be business women and also seductive women. That's why Bettie Page will never go out of style."

Todd Oldham
Fashion Designer

"I want to thank her for all the years of inspiration. How could you not admire Bettie Page? She was revolutionary. Her pictures presented women in very sexy ways but also a woman totally in control. There was not an exploitive thread in any of Bettie Page's pictures. They were reverent to her and to the celebration of woman, never smacking of 'victim.'

Bettie Page was truly skilled at knowing how to pose. She looks completely contemporary. Everything about her remains fresh. Her magic is transcendent. She was very gorgeous with an amazing sense of style — and in such a beautiful body. Really incredible. I don't think we saw a body that beautiful until Madonna — flawless but still womanly, not absurd. She had beautiful tone and a gorgeous shape — that beautiful little handful of flesh beneath her naval, that womanly belly — without being a caricature of a woman. It's a classically modern body.

Even way past her physical life on this planet she will still be with us. She is in our minds the way that Marilyn Monroe is — forever. She's had all the luxury of an icon that died."

Joey Arias
Singer, Performance Artist

"I discovered Bettie when I was quite young in my father's magazines, and I thought she was the moon child of the sex goddesses — the dark Monroe. I can relate to what she did in her time because she was thought of as subversive. What I do could be subversive, but it's just fun. And she made what she did seem as if it was just fun.

I was going to do a Coco Chanel performance at Barney's in New York, but suddenly they didn't want me to do that. They turned to me and said, 'Do someone else.' I wanted to do another strong woman, so I did Bettie Page in a Coco Chanel suit, and people went wild! So many photographers are Bettie Page fans that now I've done a series of sessions where we recreate her actual poses.

She's popular in the gay community because we're quick to spot new trends and exciting people and whatever's happening in the arts. Also, Bettie wasn't given her glory in her own time and gay people can relate to that, too. Now, finally, in the nineties, we're getting the respect we deserve. And Bettie, who has become 'the queen,' is getting her due now, too."

BETTIE PAGE

Debi Mazar
Actress

"I discovered Bettie Page when I was four-teen years old. People kept comparing me to her, so I checked her out, then ran out and got bangs! She inspired me. The girl could pose! She was ahead of her time and wasn't afraid of her sexuality."

Photos courtesy of Albert Sanchez

Janice Dickinson

Janice Dickinson paid tribute to Bettie in two guises — supermodel and photographer. In a series of self-portraits she emphasized Bettie's dominance.

"Why do I like Bettie Page? Because Bettie Page is the only institution of pin-up. She is a legend. She broke ground. Bettie Page did things in her era that set a precedent for photography, for imagery, for women. I love her passion for posing. She is A-list in my book. Bettie's dualism of innocence and sexuality perfectly represented the Fifties. But in each era, Bettie Page holds up. She holds her own. She absolutely influenced fashion. Pin-up, in fashion, is back because there is nowhere else to go.

Bettie Page was the imp of spring. Everyone loves her mischievous naughtiness. It's the mischief aspect in all of us where Bettie rules, and still does. I think it would be nice to be tied up like that. I'd love it."

Ellen von Unwerth
Photographer

Top fashion photographer Ellen von Unwerth and supermodel Eva Herzigova collaborated on a photo essay that celebrates Bettie's dualism — the naughty seductress snapping her whip and the girl next door frolicking in her leopard swimsuit.

"The secret of Bettie Page's appeal is her personality, which is not going out of fashion because she's really funny and witty and charming.

She's like Marilyn Monroe; she is never going to go out of fashion. Some women are always going to be present in our imaginations and I am sure Bettie Page is one of them.

It's her eyes and her very naughty pictures; she is so charming that everybody — women and men — likes them. That's why it's not sexist. The pictures are really nice. I wish I could have photographed her and that she could have been modeling for me, because she is exactly the kind of girl I like. I love that some of the photos look like they were taken in her own bedroom.

Lots of people are influenced by her because she really brought in a new style and fashion people always look for inspiration — designers, photographers, everybody. I'm definitely sure that people are influenced by her. I think the pin-up look will always be there. People just love to see it because it's sexy and I think sexy images are always popular. I really love Bettie's pin-up character.

I think every woman should present herself as she feels. I love sexy women. When I shot the Wonderbra campaign with Eva, for example, it was feminine and funny. Pin-ups are not vulgar. I'm against vulgarity. I like what is charming, and humorous. That's why Bettie Page is so strong and that's what is coming through. She loves what she's doing, and she does it with fun. That's why she's not a victim. There's nothing wrong with a woman in control of what she's doing.

I love it when she's completely tied up and giving a big smile to the camera. Or when she's holding a hairbrush to spank the other girls. Or when she's roller skating around Manhattan with a gorilla! It's genius, and exactly the kind of humor I love."

Eva Herzigova
Supermodel

"I was extremely flattered when Ellen asked me to pose as Bettie. She was a pioneer in 'pin-up style' and represented America and was an inspiration for future pin-up girls. She sent me her calendar in thanks for doing a good job. I was so excited! I would love to meet her someday. She has a gorgeous body and legs. She has a wonderful naiveté and innocence that makes me feel she's not 'posing' or 'acting' — it's really her. She's eternal. How many of us modeling today will be famous, or even remembered, forty years from now?"

Christy Turlington
Supermodel

Harper's Bazaar shocked readers with Peter Lindbergh's erotic photos of supermodel Christy Turlington as a black-banged Bettie Page disciple. *Harper's* suggested that wearing these clothes was as good — or better — than sex itself.

Previous page: Corset by Gianni Versace. Above: Corset top by Karl Lagerfeld. Right: Corset-style dress by Dolce & Gabbana. Photographed by Peter Lindbergh, courtesy of *Harper's Bazaar*.

Above: Girdle by Gianni Versace. Below: Halter dress by Fendi. Right: Dress by Jean Colonna. In the 1950s not one fashion magazine would dare publish a photo of Bettie Page. Today, all the fashion magazines publish photos of the top models in the fetish wear she made famous.

Supermodel Shalom Harlow adores the spirit and image of Bettie Page, and Bettie returns the compliment: "I love Shalom's sultry, mysterious look." Like her idol, Harlow possesses the riveting eyes and chameleon-like quality that made Bettie an icon.

Shalom Harlow, Supermodel

"What I like the most about Bettie's pictures is the playful quality she has. She always has it, this childlike playfulness. You can see she has a sense of humor. Sometimes it's not so subtle, but the sense of humor is always there. That's what I admire the most about her.

I think she represents what women can be now, whereas at the time, she was more of an underground cult figure. And it's only now, 40 years later, that she's being accepted by society. As a woman I think it's remarkable that she had the courage to take the plunge and do something that nobody's ever done before. She made waves in uncharted waters. That's what happens when you have a person who's so unique in her individuality — she breaks ground for other people. Women today are so much more able to express ourselves openly. I can't believe that Bettie is so modest to say that she didn't do anything important!

Look, for example, at Ellen von Unwerth's photography. It's completely Bettie Page-inspired. Where would the fashion world be without Bettie's inspiration?

Her sex appeal is undeniable. It is so obvious that to mention it sounds trite. But it's undeniable. Her figure is fantastically beautiful. I wish more women took pride in having a figure like that nowadays. It's glorious. Her body is the woman's body glorified.

But to me, it's the mixture of that sex appeal with the childlike playfulness and the sense of humor that makes her so special. Because it's never really vulgar, though it so easily could be. Bettie makes me feel proud to be a woman.

Bettie's influence on clothing is undeniable. You see the prints that she brought to fashion, the sexy styles, the lingerie. At a Dolce & Gabbana show, we were sent out with leopard prints and sheer black dresses, the Fifties hairdo, and we walked down the runway with whips. And all that was racing through my head was Bettie Page."

Demi Moore
Actress

Demi Moore plays Bettie
Page in photographer
Matthew Rolston's tribute
to a legend.

Conclusion: The Real Bettie Page

I was happy as a lark stark naked.

—Bettie Page

Bettie Page, the woman, does not acknowledge Bettie Page, the icon. To others, she is an international and timeless symbol of fashion, style and sexual freedom. To herself, she is just Bettie. "This popularity is sort of strange to me, and very surprising, but delightful! It was so long ago, and it was only seven years of my life. I thought I would be forgotten by now."

Bettie has lived in and around Southern California since 1978 — virtually in the midst of her fandom, but unaware of her fame. Though living near the entertainment capital of the world, she had no idea of the extent of her popularity. Many women of retirement age aren't familiar with the Bettie Page phenomenon, but it's ironic that Bettie herself was one of them. Occasionally a relative or friend reported seeing a picture of her, but she ignored those clues and remained uninformed of the national media search for her. She didn't even know that Dave Stevens based the female protagonist in *The Rocketeer* on her. In fact, she saw the comic book for the first time in 1993 when Stevens gave her a copy, and the film in 1994 when Hugh Hefner screened it for her at the Playboy mansion.

She never tried to disguise her identity. She kept her name, her famous bangs and her long, wavy hair. Through the years, strangers approached her occasionally in a grocery store or a shopping mall and asked if she was the famous model Bettie Page. To protect her privacy, she'd just smile and say, "Who's that?" "I was never trying to keep away from people," she says. "I was just through with modeling and went on to other things. I went right on living my life in the open all the time."

Bettie moved from her brother Jimmie's house in 1987. Since then she has lived alone and in group situations with other retirees, depending mainly on Social Security for her income. She continues to live modestly and to pursue her many interests. She reads avidly, reader, mainly non-fiction, and she still enjoys cooking and gardening as long as she doesn't have to do either early in the morning. An avowed night owl, she stays awake sometimes until dawn watching old movies on television. She still reads the Bible and goes to church when she can. Often she listens to Bible studies and church services on the radio. She has just begun exercising again after a brief lull. She likes to take long walks, though a knee injured long ago still bothers her. She has a small circle of friends, young and old, with whom she enjoys going to dinner, shopping

and, of course, to the movies. Still shunning anything other than the wholesome life, she eats only natural foods and orders nonfat milk with dinner, even at fancy restaurants.

Bettie stays abreast of current affairs and watches the entertainment and modeling scene with interest. Her favorite contemporary models include Shalom Harlow, Eva Herzigova and "that cute little blonde, Claudia Schiffer." Bette Davis remains her favorite actress, and the two films most dear to her are *Dark Victory* and the Errol Flynn version of *Robin Hood.* While no one will take the place in her mind of the legendary film stars of the past, she admires Sharon Stone for her performance in *Basic Instinct.* She enjoyed the movie *Ed Wood,* which brought back memories of the Fifties, and of a girlfriend who unknowingly married a transvestite. She loves to go out to hear live music, and recently went nightclubbing with young friends to see the singer Frankie Laine.

Now aware of her popularity, Bettie says it won't change her life. She will continue to live out of the public eye. But she is not indifferent to her fans or to her fame. She is thrilled to find out that she inspired designer Todd Oldham, that Steven Tyler of Aerosmith is one of her biggest fans, that the supermodels of today know who she is and that a famous drag queen does a Bettie Page act. She is both flattered and baffled by the worship of "the young people." And despite her lack of greed and her unwillingness to "cash in," she does look forward to some rewards. She hopes that a movie about her life — always in discussion — will finally be made, and she's considering taking up the offer of a designer and endorsing a line of clothes. She receives frequent offers to make public appearances or host events, but she'd rather preserve her privacy and be remembered as she was.

Bettie never speculates on the reasons for her iconic status: "I haven't the foggiest notion of why I'm popular. I never considered myself anything special in the looks or any other department. It's all a big mystery to me," she replies to the repeated question of why she is famous today. She offers no analysis of why she is the potentate of fetish and nude modeling, or why, out of hundreds of women who posed in her era, she endured into the modern age.

The real Bettie Page has a difficult time seeing herself as the sexual pioneer others describe. She admits to no sexual arousal while being photographed, no feeling of power in front of the camera. "I was just worried about doing a good job," she says. Yet she admits that she often pretended the camera was a man. She remembers her choice of career as a practical matter. She enjoyed the modeling because it freed her from desk jobs and it paid far more than clerical work. She won't admit that it was either a thrill or an act of defiance. Nor does she believe that she sought attention by using her sexuality because of childhood sexual abuse. In the end, she doesn't even believe that what happened with her father tainted her beliefs about sex. "I never felt like a victim because of what he did to me," she says. "I've taken it in stride." In fact, Bettie doesn't regard herself as a victim of anyone. Despite the difficulties she has faced, she is optimistic and without bitterness. "I hope my story doesn't sound morbid because of some of the things that have happened to me. I don't want people to think that. I don't feel that way at all."

Bettie forgave her father for what he did after he found religion and became a preacher. She has made her peace with him and with those memories. But she does not endorse silence about sexual abuse. She had ample time to change her mind about revealing the experience in this book, but she remained adamant. "Put it all in there," she insisted. "This is my life, both the good and the bad. I never told anyone these things and I want to get them off my chest."

She grants that her unhappy childhood affected her personal choices. Each marriage was an attempt to create the happy family experience she craved as a child. Billy Neal and Armond Walterson had close-knit families that Bettie envied, and Harry Lear provided the home and the children she always wanted. Despite three unhappy marriages and the sexual abuse, Bettie stands by her conviction that it's a woman's right to express herself sexually — whether in the bedroom or before the camera. "Women who don't express themselves sexually become repressed, and that causes them to suffer."

Though she doesn't define herself as a feminist or a rebel, Bettie welcomed the frank discussions of sex brought about by the sexual revolution. "It was about time that people talked about it, especially parents talking to their children. When I was growing up, it was so hush-hush that children were never taught anything about sex. I was frightened to death when I started menstruating at thirteen. I had no idea what was happening. I thought I was dying. I didn't know anything about sex or about protecting myself. I had to learn it the hard way. So I was glad when sex was brought out into the open. I don't like promiscuity, though. I would never have sex with a man unless I thought I was in love with him or at least liked him very much."

After her divorce from Lear, Bettie remained single and intends to stay that way. "I'm too old for all that now," she says, dismissing the possibility. But her romantic spirit is still alive. "I miss being in love," she says wistfully. "Being in love is a wonderful thing. You're very happy. You don't have any problems when you enjoy being with someone. I was always very happy when I was in love — or thought I was in love. It's a beautiful thing when two people love each other and they have sex. I highly recommend it."

Bettie Page remains a complex person,

not easily labeled or categorized — an unwitting symbol of liberated sexuality from an era in which sexual expression remained cloaked and repressed; a Southern gentlewoman delighted to admit that bondage modeling was "a ball." Like all human beings, she is full of contradictions. One could say that she always gave up too easily — with teaching, with acting, with two of her husbands. But with other things she tried too hard — with her first husband, Billy, whom she married twice and tried to convert to her religious beliefs; with trying to please every two-bit photographer in New York while ignoring better opportunities. Bettie sees no conflict between her spiritual convictions and her work as a model. "I was never ashamed. I like a good nude. I like to look at them. I was happy as a lark stark naked." But as for telling us why she did what she did, or why the world responded, she offers no insight. Thus, the real Bettie Page is an enigma to us — and to herself.

In the end, Bettie's ambivalence about her life and her fame is a key, not an impediment, to understanding her legend. The answer lies not in her life and what she makes of it, but in her look, and what she came to symbolize in spite of herself. Bettie fascinates not because of any analysis we or she might offer about her life, but because she personifies what is sexually appealing to the American psyche — middle-America soda-shop good looks with an undercurrent of sexual availability. In one body and one face, Bettie Page balanced the sexual contradictions of her time.

Bettie speaks to us in images, not in words. Even in her heyday, she granted no interviews and offered no private revelations. Her fans in the 1950s knew almost nothing about her, and herein is the key to her longevity and her universal status. Had she been more vocal, had she blurred her image with the reality of who she really was, she would not be timeless. Her fans could project any fantasy upon her. They continue to do so. The less we know, the more we can imagine.

Perhaps we ask too much of our icons when we ask them to tell us why we love them. How can they, any more than we, explain the alchemy of the perfect face at the perfect time? It's a coincidence, a one-in-a-million occurrence, and all the will and talent of makeup artists, stylists, studio publicity masters and spin doctors cannot create an icon at odds with her time. Bettie became an legend not by will, but by fate.

Fame was unlikely. She never posed for Avedon, Hurrell or the other top photographers of the day; those who shot her were either professionals on the fringe or amateurs who were often no more than shutterbug voyeurs. Dovima, Lisa Fonnsagrives and the famous fashion models became stars because of whom they worked with; Bettie Page became a star in spite of it. The "studio" was usually a shabbily furnished Broadway walk-up, not an elaborately styled professional set. She did her own makeup, set her own hair, booked her own appointments. Designers didn't offer her gowns. She designed and sewed her own dresses and swimsuits, often staying up all night before a shoot to finish an outfit. *Vogue, Harper's Bazaar* and the other important magazines never published a single photo of her.

Without calculation, Bettie made choices that distinguished her from the other pin-up models of the 1950s and earned her a place in history. While hundreds of women peroxided their hair to resemble Monroe and Mansfield, Bettie remained a brunette. In an era of heightened female artifice, she preferred a natural, casual look. Conspicuous consumption was characteristic of the post-war era, but Bettie lived, dressed and behaved simply. In comparison to the others, she worked hard to stay strong and athletic, not girdled and enhanced. As one writer pointed out, the women of the Fifties, like the food they prepared, were creamed and molded. Bettie Page was neither. She didn't pout, purr or act childlike — the favorite female characteristics of the day. She neither exaggerated her feminine charms nor assumed the role of the sexy little girl. In her thirties, at the peak of her career, she was a full-blown woman at the height of her sexual powers. Other sex symbols reflected the superficialities of sex; Bettie Page gave us what was real. Her smile, her demeanor and her appearance radiated sexual authenticity.

She never tried to create a mystique about herself, but the choices she made wrapped her in a cloak of intrigue. Always, she kept her private life out of the public eye and never sought publicity. Marilyn Monroe never passed up a photo opportunity and Jayne Mansfield was addicted to publicity stunts, but Bettie never had a publicist, manager or lawyer. She didn't align herself with famous men; her romances, marriages and divorces remained private. She never engaged in a public dispute. She kept no entourage, no advisors, no hangers-on. She gave one interview in her entire career. While Mansfield signed autographs at supermarkets around the country, rode an elephant for a crowd of 20,000 and told every reporter she met about her 163 IQ, Bettie made no public appearances. She never made the rounds to the photographers with her portfolio. She never called on movie and television producers in New York. She didn't seek fame then; she doesn't seek it now. Marilyn Monroe, the ultimate glamour girl of the 1950s, played the game and assumed the artifice, but desperately sought the public's love and the perception that she was a serious actress who read books. Bettie Page conducted her business in New York City in jeans and sweaters wearing no makeup, invisible to the public. Quietly,

she studied the Stanislavsky method and then went home — where she in fact read books.

Bettie's authenticity allowed her to transcend her time and make the transition from postwar pin-up girl to a modern symbol of female sexual independence. Modeling in the era of tease, she was solely an object of male desire. Her fans were exclusively men in search of a sexual fantasy — a forbidden sexual fantasy at that. In the 1960s sexual mores relaxed and taunting was no longer appropriate, or even attractive. Suddenly nice girls stopped using their virginity as a bargaining chip. Good girls realized what they'd been missing, how they'd been thwarted, and began to go all the way. The promise of sex without delivery was outdated; female sexual power was in, and pin-up queens like Jayne Mansfield were relegated to nostalgia as the culture passed them by. If tease had been Bettie's only appeal, she might have gone out of style. As it is, she continues to influence style.

Today she is embraced by women as well as men. As women abandon sexual passivity and compliance, Bettie Page, who embraced the provocative and the experimental, has become an enduring symbol of female independence and genuineness. Her indelible imprint on the hearts and minds of her fans, and on the culture at large, will never go away. One way or another, she will be with us for a long, long time.

As much as we can know any new friend, we now know the real Bettie Page. We've grown to love her, but we've given up trying to convince her that she's a legend. Perhaps someday she will understand the place she holds in other people's lives, hopes and fantasies. In the meantime, we continue to enjoy her friendship.

When the exhausting week of interviews was over, Bettie wanted to celebrate with a long drive. She still loves getting in a car and

"just driving," as she did with Tony Campo a long time ago. She hadn't been to Hollywood in years — would we take her there? We stopped for a late lunch in town and then drove to Santa Monica so she could see the ocean. We walked to the end of the pier to watch the sunset and laughed at what we found there: a photographer with his model catching the day's last light. Magic hour. "How about a picture, Bettie?" we teased. "Forget it! You'll have to rely on your memory." As we watched her lean against the railing, toss her hair in the wind and watch the sun slip below the sea, we remembered her vow: never to be photographed again, not for our scrapbooks, not for this book. Yet she was still there. The face we saw — the face the public has not seen in nearly 40 years — is still the face of an icon. Not because she looks the same. Not because she didn't grow old. But because the real Bettie Page never confused herself with the woman in the photos. She didn't manufacture a false persona and spend the rest of her life failing to live up to it. She never tried to become a different person for the camera. Instead, she let the pictures capture the woman she always was.

Source Guide

A Checklist for Bettie Page Fans

BETTIE PAGE AUTOGRAPHS: Copies of *Bettie Page: The Life of a Pin-Up Legend* signed by Bettie are available exclusively from Glamourcon, Inc. ($49.95 plus $4.00 shipping), as are signed photographs, calendars, trading cards, a video documentary and *Fond Memories*, the official Bettie Page fanzine. Glamourcon offers only authorized material and Bettie receives a royalty on all sales. Twice each year Glamourcon sponsors a collector's festival celebrating American pin-up art and memorabilia. Glamourcon, Dept. BP, P.O. Box 2594, Woodinville, WA 98072. Telephone: (206) 821-1760, Fax: (206) 821-8274, Internet glamourcon @ AOL.com.

ROBERT BLUE: Original oil paintings and limited edition prints are available from Glamourcon, Inc.

PLAYBOY CENTERFOLD: The January, 1955 centerfold on page 141 is available in a limited edition of 750 museum quality prints signed by Hugh M. Hefner and Bettie Page. To order, call David Oates at Playboy Special Editions, (312) 751-8000.

OLIVIA: Paintings, prints, books, trading cards and calendars are available from Ozone Productions Ltd., P. O. Box 4153, Point Dume Station, Malibu, CA 90265. Notecards are available from O Card Corp., P. O. Box 111, Rosyln, NY 11576.

CLAYBURN MOORE: The bronze sculpture on page 237, cast in a limited edition of 50, is available from Moore Creations, P. O. Box 202137, Austin, TX 78720. Telephone: (512) 219-7297. Fax: (512) 219-7357.

SHEL-TONE: A boxed set of trading cards depicting the 3-D photos of Bettie from the camera club chapter is available from Shel-Tone Publications, P. O. Box 45, Irvington, NJ 07111.

DAVE STEVENS: Posters and limited edition prints are available from Glamourcon, Inc.

KITCHEN SINK PRESS: A quality company that produces a number of Bettie Page items, including trading cards, metal signs, 1950s thermometers, a reprint of the scarce *Private Peeks* series and the long-awaited official Bettie Page candy bar. To request a catalog, write to Kitchen Sink Press, Dept. BP, 320 Riverside Dr., Northhampton, MA 01060.

MOVIE STAR NEWS: Original Klaw photos and remastered loops on tape are available from Movie Star News, 134 W. 18th Street, New York, NY 10011.

AUTHORS' REQUEST

The authors solicit your help for a second volume of this book. Did you know Bettie Page? Did you photograph her? Do you own unpublished Bettie Page photographs? Do you have Bettie Page ephemera — fugitive newspaper clippings, playbills, unusual collectibles? Films, tapes or kinescopes of her television appearances? Posters and ads from her film and print appearances?

Did you know Irving Klaw? Were you a customer of Movie Star News in the 1950s? Did you model for Irving Klaw? Do you own vintage Klaw prints or catalogues of Bettie Page or other models? The authors seek materials and anecdotes.

We also seek documents, photos and archives from the 1950s mens' magazines, including negatives or prints by Jan Caldwell, Bill Hamilton, Weegee, Correa and other 1950s pin-up photographers.

Please write to the authors at P. O. Box 56176, Chicago, IL 60656

Index

In this post-modern era, we turn to science to give the last word on a pop culture phenomenon — Bettie Page's eternal appeal. Professor Michael Cunningham, a psychologist who studies facial appearance says this:

"I took nine measurements of Bettie Page's features using an electronic micrometer, and then standardized those measures as ratios to the size of the head. I compared Bettie's facialmetrics to a database containing measurements of both other stars and of uncelebrated women. The numbers confirmed what most pin-up viewers might intuitively perceive.

The height and width of Bettie Page's eyes were much greater than average, giving her the appearance of child-like innocence and playfulness. That effect was compounded by her very large smile, and her eyebrows, which were set higher than average. The combination of child-like and expressive features made her face appear open and non-threatening.

Had Bettie's cheekbones and chin been larger, she might have seemed intimidatingly beautiful. But those features were in the normal range, so the overall appearance is not that of an unobtainable ice-princess, but rather that of a pleasant and eager-to-please girl next door.

Bettie's long-term appeal may be due, in part, to the contrast between her facial appearance and that of her body and apparel. Her face gives the impression of a sweet and wholesome girl who would not turn a guy down for a date, or make him feel inadequate. At the same time, her black lace and sensuous pose suggest that the date will not be limited to a chat at the malt shop and a chaste kiss at the door. The perception of sweetness and sexuality, of pleasure without threat, may capture the heart of the ambivalent 20th Century American man."

Bettie Page Facialmetrics:

Height of eye ratio	.08
Width of eye ratio	.29
Height of smile ratio	.05
Width of smile ratio	.59
Height of eyebrow ratio	.05
Prominence of cheekbones	.11